Characters by the Bushel

Joe Culver

Tommy Adams,
A coon-hunting
buddy. Enjoy the
stories.

DEDICATION

This book is dedicated to Herman and Pod Tilley, who raised their family on the farm in Monkey's Eyebrow where I now live. For many of us, "coming home" meant visiting Pod and Herman.

It's also dedicated to the memory of Bill Ryan of Wickliffe, father of my best friend Danny Ryan. If Bill's filling station had not been a place where characters gathered, I probably would not have heard most of the stories in this book.

CONTENTS

1 TALES FROM BILL RYAN'S STATION

Danny Ryan was my best friend when we were growing up in the small (population 900 back then) town of Wickliffe, on the extreme western tip of Kentucky where the Ohio flows into the Mississippi River.

His father, Bill Ryan, ran the Standard Oil filling station, where many of the town's characters gathered to outdo each other in the unofficial competition of storytelling and creating colorful expressions.

Bill was one of the best at coming up with short, very funny statements to make a point in such a way as to etch them indelibly on my young brain.

About as broke as you could be

You've heard people say, "I'm so broke I can't pay attention." That's been said so much that it's a cliché. People in Ballard County didn't need clichés. The culture demanded originality.

For instance, the people lounging – that's a polite term for loafing – around Bill Ryan's service station in Wickliffe were taking turns bemoaning their respective states of finance. "Can't pay attention" would not have been a part of this discussion in Wickliffe. Too trite.

Bill topped them all with this description of how bad off he was: "If turkey was selling for a nickel a pound, I couldn't kiss a hummin'bird's ass."

Breaking even

It was a slow day at Bill Ryan's station.

A tourist pulled up to the service station. He said he didn't need any gas, just wanted to use the bathroom.

He used the bathroom and then took a long drink of cold water from the fountain. Then, he pulled out a dollar and asked for change, and, as usual, Bill obliged.

The tourist then asked, "How's business?"

Bill replied, "Well, I'm swapping ice water for piss and breaking even on change. I guess I'm doing all right."

A scarcity of gazelles

Danny Ryan and I were no longer children. Danny was living in the Jonathan Creek area of Kentucky Lake. Grown up and holding a good job, Danny decided he needed to add some sophistication, something we might call "putting on airs."

Sophistication for Danny included the purchase of an Afghan hound, a beautiful, sleek, longhaired dog you probably see more often in dog shows than in dog houses.

"Son," Bill told him, "I just can't understand why you would buy something as useless as an

Afghan hound when you could have bought a
Chesapeake Bay retriever or a Lab that you could
take duck hunting."

"But dad," Danny defended, "Afghans aren't
useless. Why, they use them in Africa to hunt
gazelles."

"Well son, that's wonderful," Bill growled at
Danny, "but sometimes I go two, maybe three
days and not see a gazelle."

Colorful and off-colorful expressions

Banter from Bill Ryan's service station: "Did
you just fart?" "Hell yes, you don't think I smell
this way all the time, do ya?"

Someone loafing at Bill Ryan's station
described the soil in the river bottoms after the
backwater went down as being "as rich as three
feet up a bull's ass."

Tim Hughes, son of Urban Hughes about whom
the tales assume mythical proportions, passed
along these:

Someone describing a cross-eyed person: "He's
a little tangle-eyed. I think he was born in the
middle of the week lookin' both ways for Sunday."

Regarding bad luck, Tim heard this from a
black woman who was shopping in his father's
store: "I'm so far down that bottom looks like up."

Tim says he first heard this saying from a
friend referring to some young lady walking down
the sidewalk: "Her ass looks like two pipe stems
stuck in a pumpkin."

In reference to the deceased at a funeral: "Putting a suit on that old fart is like installing an elevator in an outhouse."

Danny Ryan passes along this statement by Urban Hughes, when Joe Garrett was walking past Bill Ryan's station. Mr. Garrett was my cousin George Crice's grandfather and had a nose of prodigious proportions. As Mr. Garrett walked by, Urban turned to Danny, "How would you like to have his nose full of nickels?"

Red Harrington (another character about whom the tales abound) while taking a leak at Prairie Lake in the river bottoms, and speaking to his manhood: "Well old pal, we've had a lot of good times together, but I've just outlived ya."

It was a dry summer and farmers were congregating in and around Bill Ryan's station, praying for rain, wondering aloud when it would rain, etc. Tired of all the talk, Red Harrington said, "I hope they get so much rain that the knob on the courthouse door looks like a fishing cork."

Here are a couple more Danny Ryan tells on Red Harrington:

Reworking the phrase that someone is high, wide and handsome, Red said of a man rather large in the rear, "He's high, wide and ass-some."

Bill Ryan and Homer Lee Elliott were bragging on each other for going without a drink. Homer Lee said he hadn't had a drink in a week. Bill said now that he thought about it, he hadn't had one in two or three weeks. Red Harrington ended that brag session: "I turned down one drink in my life and I've been sorry ever since."

Here's one from Tommy Ryan, quoting Joe Wear of the Rudd-Wear Drug Store: "Son, there's more horses asses in this world than there are horses."

It was a bad spring for mosquitoes. Gabe Cullen was covered up by them down in the river bottoms. Someone said he should swat them away. "Aw, I'll just leave them alone. They'll get their fill and leave."

It would be a long walk, B. Allie

B. Allie Hall was another Wickliffe resident who made it into quite a few stories.

He achieved a certain degree of fame for working anonymously to acquire property on behalf of the Westvaco Corporation, which built a paper mill between Wickliffe and Bardwell, and which remains today as one of the county's main employers, although under a different name.

B. Allie was a surveyor and he also cruised timber. To cruise timber is to take various measurements and then come up with an estimate of the amount of timber in a given forest. This helps set a value on the timber.

B. Allie and Bill Ryan were in the bottoms for something, possibly hunting squirrels. When it was time to go back to their vehicle, they had a disagreement over which way to go.

B. Allie declared that he had cruised timber in these woods and knew they had to go that way.

"Well by God, B. Allie," Bill replied, "yes, you can get back going that way. Trouble is, you have to walk all the way around the world to do it!"

When my uncle Billy Bob Crice was elected sheriff of Ballard County not long after he had been drafted into the army, he hired B. Allie as his chief deputy to run the sheriff's office until Billy Bob served out his military term.

When Billy Bob installed the county's first two-way radio, B. Allie frequently was the operator of the base unit in the sheriff's office.

B. Allie had a huge, booming voice. When he used the radio, he took full advantage of his voice.

Folks laughed that he didn't need a radio. Billy Bob could have heard that voice anywhere in the county.

It's easy to be humble if you're rooted in ... well, read on

Not that I have any special justification for feeling better than anyone else, but from time to time my head has increased a couple of cap sizes and I feel pretty proud of what I've accomplished over the years.

But before I'm in real danger of floating too far off the ground, Bill Ryan brings me down to earth.

Yes, Bill has been dead for many years, but his sayings, his attitude, his creativity remain with me. And I'm about to tell you what he said one day that keeps me rooted firmly in who I am and where I came from.

Bill had business with the Standard Oil distributor in Paducah one day and he let Danny and me ride with him.

We were met by a receptionist or secretary. In retrospect, I think her assignment was to do her best to keep people from intruding on the boss. She was there to keep out the riff raff.

Bill told her he was there to see the distributor.

He had to prove his worthiness before she would let him pass.

"Do you have an appointment?" "What is the nature of your business?" "Is he expecting you?"

Those were the types of questions she asked before she would allow Bill to pass.

Finally, Bill had established the proper level of credibility and the inquisitor accepted the fact that he should be allowed into the executive area.

"And whom shall I say is calling?" she sniffed her final question.

I still regard what Bill said as one of the great answers of all time:

"Bill Ryan, just as common as cat shit."

Today, if I discover myself feeling a little uppity, I think about that answer and what it means on many different levels.

You could regard it as a sarcastic, impatient response to an unnecessary level of interrogation.

I prefer to regard it as a reflection of a person who knows who he is, is satisfied with knowing and being that person, and who doesn't need a façade that might suggest anything beyond that.

What you see is what you get.

In my experience, it's hard not to be humble when you know you're firmly rooted in a litter box.

How to spray a wasp

Everett Hughes was one of the regular hangers-on at Bill Ryan's station.

Bill had a cabin on Prairie Lake in the river bottoms outside of Wickliffe. It wasn't unusual for a few wasps to find their way inside the cabin, so one of the staples was a can of Raid or Black Flag wasp spray.

Everett and Bill had driven Bill's late-50 Dodge truck into the bottoms on this particular day to do something at the cabin.

Sure enough, they were greeted by wasps.

Everett said he would get rid of them, so he grabbed the can of bug spray, and chased around the cabin for a few seconds until one of the wasps had settled down into a place where he could spray it effectively.

He aimed the wasp spray carefully, and mashed the spray button.

Trouble was, he hadn't bothered to make sure the nozzle was pointing toward the wasp. It didn't take him more than a second or two to realize that it was aimed directly at his face. Had the wasp been sitting on his nose, it would have received a lethal dose.

Butter up!

Bill Ryan took his two sons, Danny and Tommy, and Everett Hughes to St. Louis to watch a Cardinals' baseball game.

They stopped at a restaurant for dinner before the game.

Everett either wasn't paying attention or he had some vision trouble during dinner because when he reached for a cracker, he grabbed a pat of butter instead and got it all over his fingers.

At the game later, Everett, a hard-core Cardinals' fan (as were many of the people in our small town), was laying into the home plate umpire for his balls and strikes calls.

Finally Bill couldn't keep quiet any longer. He turned to Everett, "Just how in the hell is it that you can see those home plate corners better than the ump when you couldn't even tell a pat of butter from a cracker!"

When Danny took requests

Danny Ryan and I were teenagers in the early days of rock and roll, and at the beginning of what would later be called soul music.

I tried to play guitar, with limited success, but knew better than to try to sing. My talent as a singer ranks right up near the top of the worst singing voices ever.

Danny, meanwhile, got a ukulele.

His voice wasn't much better than mine, but either he didn't realize that or he capitalized on it in his ongoing effort to draw out responses from his dad, Bill Ryan.

Danny hung out at Bill's gas station and worked occasionally, particularly on weekends and during the summer.

I just hung out there, enjoying Danny's company and loving the stories that Bill and others of his age – who also hung out at the station – told.

Danny usually had the ukulele with him, and his playing and singing consistently drew grimaces and other responses from Bill.

Danny was going through a stage when he would aggravate his dad by referring to him as "Dad babe."

On this particular day, Danny managed to evoke a classic Bill Ryan response.

Having caused several minutes of pain and grimace with his playing and singing, Danny baited Bill with the question: "Hey Dad babe, whadaya want me to play?"

Bill's three word answer summed it all up:

"Play dead son."

A good reason to go armed

Tot Waldon told me this story from Bill Ryan's Service Station.

The way Tot heard the story, Pug Hammett or maybe it was Ham Stroud of Wickliffe ran for sheriff of Ballard County. This was back in the days when voters marked an X in pencil beside the name of the candidate they wanted to vote for.

Ballot boxes had to be brought from each precinct to the courthouse at Wickliffe and the ballots were counted one at a time. Sometimes – in fact, usually – the process took several hours and candidates and voters tended to get restless.

Counting was delayed on this night because one of the election officials who had a key needed to open the ballot boxes was out of town.

Determined that no one would get a chance to stuff a ballot box, Pug or Ham – according to the story – went home, got a shotgun and came back to the courthouse where he spent the night guarding the ballot boxes.

When the votes finally were counted, the candidate had received only 75 votes.

He took his shotgun, went home, put down the shotgun, picked up a pistol and either stuck it in a holster or put it in his pants.

When the candidate and his pistol showed up at Bill's station, the regulars who gathered there expressed their regrets at the paltry number of votes he had received, and they asked him why he was carrying the pistol.

"Hell, boys, when you ain't got any more friends than I have, you'd better go armed," he is supposed to have said.

The gag that gagged

Danny Ryan and I were in high school, so that places this story in the late 1950s or early '60s.

It takes place – where else – in Bill Ryan's Standard Oil gas station.

On this particular day, at this particular time, Bill wasn't there. Danny was running the station and I was there, too.

A couple of days earlier, Danny bought a puke pad. It was made of rubber or plastic, perhaps six inches in diameter, and looked very realistic, just as if someone had lost his or her dinner.

There was a water fountain inside the station and Danny thought it would make a great gag to put the pad in the bottom of the fountain.

It wasn't long before one of the regulars showed up. I think it might have been Homer Lee Elliott. He caught a glimpse of the pad in the fountain.

"Damn, someone threw up in the water fountain," he informed us.

Danny walked over and looked at it as if he wasn't aware.

He backed up quickly and made some gagging sounds.

"You need to clean that up," Homer Lee told Danny.

"I can't," Danny said. "It makes me sick to look at it. If I tried to clean that up I would wind up vomiting myself. Can you do it?"

Grumbling and with great reluctance, he said he would.

He got a paper towel, approached the fountain with some trepidation, and gingerly reached out toward the pad.

When he got the towel in place, he tried to scoop up some of the "vomit." The entire pad moved at that time of course, and as he kept trying to scoop it, he raised one side of the pad completely off the bottom of the fountain.

"My God, how long has this been in here!" he demanded between the gagging noises he was making. "It's set so long that it has turned solid!"

That did it. Danny and I cracked up at that point.

Homer Lee realized what was going on and he wasn't any too happy with us, but such was life at Bill Ryan's station.

2 MONKEY'S EYEBROW AND VICINITY

I love Monkey's Eyebrow, Ky. The love affair goes back to when I was a small child and would visit Pod and Herman Tilley here during the summer. They raised their family on a farm that eventually grew to a hundred acres. People today can't make a living on a farm that small. I bought six acres from my cousin Barbara Lynn Tilley Moss, who is Pod and Herman's daughter. My property – Joe's Place – includes the land, the house, a tobacco barn, the building where Herman milked cows, and four other outbuildings. These stories are about people and events in Monkey's Eyebrow and nearby.

A Pod by any other name

I never called her anything but Pod. That's what everyone else called her too. Well, that's not exactly true. Her mother – my maternal grandmother – called her something that sounded like Margry.

But that wasn't unusual. My grandmother had her own way of saying lots of things. Maybe "her own way" is an exaggeration. At that time, in rural West Kentucky, lots of folks pronounced some words in ways that might not follow the strict guidelines of proper English.

Pod was one of the 10 children of Bob and Lannie Crice. My mother, Jessie Lee, was another. Other children were Elwood, Gene, Ann, Thelma, Nellie, Dick, Billy Bob and Anita Faye (or Nita Faye because no one pronounced the A).

And Billy Bob wasn't really Billy Bob. He was named Ernest Wells but called Billy Bob. Stories I've heard say that was because of some disagreement about what to name him, so they compromised by naming him one thing but calling him the other. I don't know if that's true.

Eventually Pod married Herman Tilley and they bought the farm at Monkey's Eyebrow, a small part of which I now own. Grandmother lived with them in the later years of her life, and she continued to call Pod Margry.

I wondered if that was grandmother's way of saying Margaret or perhaps Marguerite. Pod gave her proper name as Margaret.

Later in Pod's life she had occasion to need a birth certificate. Back in those days it was fairly common for folks not to have a copy of a birth certificate. Official records were not treated as the big deal they are now.

Pod sent off to get a copy of her birth certificate and lo and behold when it arrived, her name was listed as Margaree.

Pod wasn't sure if that was what grandmother intended to name her or if the person who filled out the birth certificate just spelled it the way grandmother said it.

She had her name legally changed to Margaret. But I like Pod better.

I don't know where she got that name, but it seemed to fit her for some reason.

Names aren't as important as people anyway.

Whether you called her Pod or Margaree or Margaret, the house she and Herman turned into a home for themselves and their two children, Barbara and Frankie, was the magnet that drew family members together.

It was a place where you felt welcome and a part of a large family of grandmother and aunts and uncles and lots of cousins.

I have very warm feelings of the home where I was raised by my parents, but for some reason that's not where I wanted to return after I retired. I wanted to move to Monkey's Eyebrow where Pod and Herman had lived. I thought maybe I could get an acre or two of land and put a house there to live.

When I asked Barbie about possibly buying part of the Tilley farm, which she and her husband Joe own after the death of Pod and Herman, they agreed to sell it to me and that's Joe's Place now.

Except it really isn't. It's still Pod and Herman's. I just get the chance to live in it and hope the memories and the love and the warmth are still embedded in the structure, and that, unlike the saying, I can go home again.

The Arivett family of Monkey's Eyebrow and other settlers of the area

(This is based on conversations with Evelyn Hook Arivett and Leroy Arivett on May 21, 2010, and on some e-mails from Evelyn and her daughter, Wilma Hook Romatz, who lives in Michigan.)

Ples and Irene Wildharber Arivett and Ples' brother Brad weren't the first people to own a business at Monkey's Eyebrow, Kentucky, but their businesses and their presence in the area are inextricably linked to the history of this small community that sports one of the most unusual names in the United States.

The name is frequently featured in atlas listings of unusual names; it has been the subject of at least two features on National Public Radio, and is featured in two books by author Mark Usler, who came to Monkey's Eyebrow on May 21 to launch his new book, Hometown Celebrations.

The Arivett name itself is also a bit unusual in that it is consistently spelled Arivett, but is pronounced three different ways within the same family. Most of the members of the family and the people who live in the area pronounce the name as Everett, but Evelyn Arivett Hook, daughter of Ples and Irene, pronounces it as it's spelled, Ar-i-vett. Evelyn's younger brother, Leroy, who lives near Chicago, pronounces it Ar-vett, without the "i" sound.

Evelyn Arivett was born at Monkey's Eyebrow in 1920, the first of four children born to Ples and Irene. Horace, who ran a store at Bandana and who died in Bandana a few years ago, was next. Then came Leroy, and finally Harold, who lives near Atlanta.

The family's roots in Monkey's Eyebrow stretch back into the 1800s.

The Wildharbers and Goodleys, Irene Arivett's family, came to Ballard County in 1903 from Henderson, Kentucky. Ples Arivett's sister, Maude, told Evelyn that when their great grandfather, Jesse Beeler, came to Ballard County from Tennessee in the early 1840s it was nothing but wilderness. For many years, he and his children all lived in houses along what is now called Monkey's Eyebrow Road, or state route 473.

"Maudie was quite a colorful character too," Wilma Hook Romatz, Evelyn's daughter, remembers, "chewing snuff and spitting into a Calumet baking powder can. She had coal black dyed hair, and a huge diamond ring and red-painted nails. Her language was equally colorful."

According to Evelyn, "Aunt Maudie said she heard that her grandpa had a whole trunk full of confederate money and her grandma kept trying to get him to change it. He refused, and lost everything after the Civil War was over."

John William Arivett, Ples Arivett's grandfather, was born in Virginia but moved to

Ballard County in the 1860s. He lived to be 98 and was married three times. He lived in Wickliffe when he died in 1940.

The business history of Monkey's Eyebrow goes back to before the Arivetts opened their first business, which was a gristmill. A man whose last name was Ray had Ray's Store at the bottom of the hill, down in an area which some folks call Old Monkey. Later, Guy Borden ran the store. Ples and Irene Arivett lived in a house near that store, on the south side of the road. There are no buildings there today. The area is covered with trees.

Several families lived in the area. Before the road was paved, the old road made a 90-degree turn to the north, opposite what is now Palmore Road, then it curved back toward the west, behind where Jim and Jean Meadors live now. The Arivett Store and most of the residences were northwest of the Meadors' house. The buildings are no longer there.

Charley Waldon lived across the field (no paved road then) south of the store in the white house where Imogene Alexander lived until she died.

A family of Beelers lived down the road. Evelyn's grandfather, John Wildharber, at one time owned the farm due east of the old road, a farm later owned by a Graves family and then by Herman and Pod Tilley, a part of which is now owned by Joe Culver.

According to Evelyn Hook, Wildharber came here from California, lived here two or three

years, and then went back. He played in a band,
When he came here he built a box that his bass
fiddle would fit into. He put the box on the back of
the car and brought it here with him.

The house where Charley Waldon's family lived
– where twin brothers Dot and Tot were born –
was previously occupied by a family named Moss.
Evelyn remembers playing with their daughter,
who was about her age.

Some other families who lived in the area were
Redferns, Crabtrees and Yanceys. "And there
were Turners who lived down there. They used to
sell watermelons. Sand Ridge grew the best
watermelons," Evelyn Hook recalls.

"There used to be some Laniers who lived down
there. Judy Magee was a Hayden, and when you
go by the game reserve entry there and you go on
down to that curve, the Haydens lived in the
house just on that curve. That's where Judy and
her sister grew up," Evelyn said.

There was a small school "right over there in
front of where that antenna is," Evelyn said,
pointing to the WPSD TV tower. "There used to
be a building that was still there when they built
the tower. I don't know if it still is. I haven't been
down that road for a while. The building was still
there even after they built that antenna out
there.

"It was called Graves School. I would say 25 or
30 children went there. It had been built for a
two-room school but we used only one of the
rooms. If it was good weather we'd play outside,

but if it was bad we could go in there, in the other room, and play games or whatever.

"The teacher that we had was real good to read to us. We used to have box suppers and she would use the money that we made from the suppers and other activities to buy books and things to entertain the kids. I love books still, and I'm sure I got it from her. Her name was Laura Lee Holt."

The Monkey's Eyebrow children went to high school at Bandana. There were no school buses then, but Howard Owsley, Joe Owsley's dad, took a two-ton flatbed truck and converted it into a bus. It was closed in, with benches around the walls and a bench down the middle. It also had windows.

"He charged us 10 cents a day," Evelyn recalls. "He would take us to Bandana and then pick us up at the end of the day. There were 15 or 20 people who rode it. He started at Needmore and drove all around the area picking up children."

Before he built the gristmill which he and his brother Brad ran, Ples Arivett worked in California twice. He also worked on Dam 53 when it was being built, when Evelyn was about four or five years old. The Arivett family lived at the bottom of the hill then, in a house just past Ray's Store.

Leroy Arivett recalls that his father would get up very early in the morning and walk the five miles to where they were building the dam. Because he left before daylight, Ples would carry a lantern. Evelyn said he would walk down to where the wildlife refuge is now, cross a lake and go over to where the dam was. Evelyn says she was born in 1920 and that would have been around 1925.

"And then we went to California in 1926," Evelyn remembers. "My dad and my uncle were working out in the oilfields. I guess the oil company owned houses and rented them to the people who worked for them. We lived out there in a mountainous area and my dad wouldn't let me go to school because he said you'll have to ride the bus and there's all those winding roads. He was afraid for me to ride the bus. So I didn't go to school until I was seven years old after we moved back."

They lived in Paducah for about a year or so and Evelyn's first year of school was in Paducah. After that, she finished grade school at the Graves School at Monkey's Eyebrow. That school remained active until it was consolidated with Bandana.

She went away to college at Murray State in the fall of 1938 and didn't move back.

The Arivetts did some farming in addition to running their businesses. Wilma taped a conversation with her uncle Horace a few years ago when he talked about the time they raised acres of sweet potatoes during the depression, thinking that they could sell them and make a little bit of money. They found it was going to cost more to ship them than they would get, so they brought them back home and ate them all winter. Horace said he still couldn't look at a sweet potato years later.

The Arivetts' first business enterprise at Monkey's Eyebrow was a gristmill operated by brothers Ples and Brad. Evelyn says she was always fascinated with the machinery at the mill. They had a tractor chassis in the back part of the mill. It had a big drive shaft that went all the way across and the motor would run an assortment of pulleys and belts. It had a crusher that crushed the corn and there was another grinder that made meal.

"The mill made a lot of meal," Evelyn says. "My dad usually did that. The Yopp Seed Company in Paducah would buy bags and let my dad fill them up with meal and they would take them back and sell them with Yopp's name on the bags."

About a year after they built the gristmill they started putting groceries in the front part. When Evelyn was about 12, in the early 1930s, the Arivetts built a frame building to house the store, separate from the mill.

There was a set of scales between the store and the mill.

Farmers would weigh their loaded trucks before the corn was ground. They would weigh them again when the trucks were empty. The difference was the weight of the corn.

Evelyn remembers that the store had about anything that you would want to buy, except meat because there was no electricity to run a cooler to keep meat.

Later, after the Arivett brothers dissolved their partnership, Ples tore down the frame building and built a new store of blocks in the same location as the first store. Those stores were on top of the hill, a location some people call "New Monkey" to distinguish it from the Ray's Store that stood at the bottom of the hill. With the advent of electricity, that store was able to sell meat.

The Arivetts ran that store until around 1955 when they retired and moved to Bandana, where Horace already had a store.

By the time the uranium enrichment plant was being built near Kevil in the 1950s, there were 14 people living beside or around the Arivetts' house and store in Monkey's Eyebrow.

When the state of Kentucky acquired several of the lakes in the area, Ples fixed up rooms to rent to hunters. "He was always looking for ways to make more business," Evelyn says.

Evelyn moved away in 1938 to go to college at Murray State. She married Harold Hook in 1942, and they lived in McCracken County, but came back to Monkey's Eyebrow often to visit her family.

She and Harold had a store for about three years in Camelia, where the road from the Paducah Airport intersects with Highway 62.

Ples Arivett died in 1975, and Irene lived until 1999. She was 96 years old.

Come in Bossie, it's time to milk

One of my favorite things to do when I visited Pod and Herman at their Monkey's Eyebrow farm was to go with Herman to his dairy barn and watch him milk.

Later, I came to look upon dairy farming as being more like a sentence than a job because it was so confining. Pod and Herman rarely went anywhere except during the middle of a day. That's because cows have to be milked each morning and each evening, seven days a week, 365 days a year and 366 days on Leap Year.

But to a kid it was something fun to watch.

I think when Herman first went into farming after the war – that would be the big war, WWII—he milked jersey cows by hand. You had to have a lot of pull to be a dairy farmer at that time. During that period he also kept mules, a sort of grain-fed, pre-tractor plow puller.

I'm not all that familiar with farm economics, but I think Herman earned most of his cash money from the milk and from the annual tobacco sale.

I recall that he also grew corn, but I think he used most of that to feed his cows. I remember going with him a time or two to the mill in Bandana where he had corn stalks and kernels ground into feed. Later, folks started growing soybeans instead of corn. I suppose the soybeans brought in more money.

Herman eventually graduated from jersey cows to holsteins, which gave much more milk per cow, and he gave up the finger-pull technique in favor of automatic milkers.

His relatively small dairy operation allowed him to bring in four cows at a time. He could milk two of them while the other two munched on the feed he shoveled into the trough in front of each cow.

The cats always showed up at milking time and Herman poured them some milk out of the shiny bucket that the milking machine filled. Then he poured the rest of the milk into the cooler where it was kept cool until the milk truck came around and picked it up.

A shovel always leaned against the wall within convenient reach because cows aren't especially particular about where and when they deposit manure. Shoveling up behind them was part of the operation.

The smells – cows, cow manure, feed – and the sounds – cows chewing, horseflies buzzing, shovel scooping, milk machine milking – are a big part of my memories. And Herman in constant motion is another memory, scooping grain into the trough (something I got to help with from time to time), wiping down the cows' udders, attaching the milkers, emptying the bucket when it was full, closing the neck clamp when the next set of cows came in, opening it when a cow had been milked, scooping when necessary, swatting horseflies, and finally cleaning up the little barn after it was all done for that morning or evening.

But the really fascinating part of it to me was how the cows knew when it was their turn and which stall was theirs. They would be standing in front of the dairy barn most of the time when it was time for milking. Sometimes we had to go into the fields and call them.

When Herman opened up the barn doors, four cows would come in. Always the same four cows. Each cow would plod to a milk station, always the same station for each cow. When two had been milked and released, two more would walk in, always in the same order and always to the same stall.

I suppose it's not odd that a cow would have enough sense to fall into a pattern. But to me, that was an amazing thing and one of the wonders of visiting Herman and Pod at Monkey's Eyebrow.

Learning the comfort of family

Our family gatherings at Pod and Herman's farm in Monkey's Eyebrow were the marks on the door frame that measured evolving family hierarchy.

Family in those days meant my mother's family. My maternal grandparents, Bob and Lannie Crice, had 10 children and they each had children. My paternal grandfather, John Culver, died before I knew him. He and my grandmother,

Edna Jones Culver, had only two children, uncle Johnny and my dad. There was also a half-brother, Charles Culver, in Lovelaceville, but we didn't visit frequently with the Culver side.

That's partly because there were so few of them. Uncle Johnny owned a business in Jonesboro, Ark., where he and his wife had only one child. Charles Culver had two children and we visited occasionally, but not frequently.

The much larger Crice family was the extended family. There were aunts and uncles and lots of cousins. This was after the fertile years during and following World War II.

We visited individual aunts and uncles and their families, of course, but when there was a larger family gathering it was usually at Pod and Herman's. Pod was one of mother's sisters. She married Herman Tilley and they raised their two children on the farm where I now own the house, barn and six acres.

It was – and is – a small house, but the walls seemed to expand when the family got together. There was always room enough and food enough for all of us.

It was at those get-togethers where we truly got to know our aunts and our uncles, our many cousins. We learned that we were part of something bigger than our parents and our brothers and sisters; we were part of a family. And even if it wasn't something we were aware of learning, we took comfort in it, even if we didn't realize we were taking comfort.

We were part of a family. We cared about each other. We enjoyed being surrounded by so many people with whom we had a genetic connection that stretched back who knows how far.

In retrospect, I believe it was at those gatherings where we measured our maturation, our growth within the family.

Just as my parents and yours, too, I'm sure, marked our vertical growth in pencil on a door frame, each mark a little higher than the one from several months ago, those gatherings marked our growth within the family.

We started out sitting at a card table with the youngest cousins. As we got older, we moved up to more grown-up tables, and we moved up in which pieces of chicken were available to us. We grew to where we were allowed to fill our own plates instead of having a parent or an aunt or an uncle fill them for us.

We moved up in intellect where the older members of the family might even let us join in the grown-up conversations.

But as we grew, the concept of family remained essentially the same because it had been powerful and flexible and expandable from the very start.

Not all the aunts and uncles and cousins were there every time. One aunt lived in Louisville, Ky. Another lived in Oak Ridge, Tenn. It was a rare occasion when they came but it was an oh so special time, too, because the family seemed to grow just a bit when they came.

Later, when jobs took some of us away from Ballard County, we didn't get together very often. But every time I made it back home, I went to visit Pod and Herman and their house of warmth and memories. I was an adult, then, and we talked as equals. Pod always had a meal when I visited. I got to sit at the big table.

Someone wrote that you can't go home again, but you can insert yourself into the cocoon of memories that saturate the walls of home. That's where I plan to live my final years.

A grocery store on wheels

One of the highlights when I spent part of the summers here in Monkey's Eyebrow when my late uncle and aunt, Herman and Pod Tilley, owned the farm where I live was when the huckster came.

The "huckster" was a merchant who drove the dusty gravel roads back in the "old days," maybe as early as the 1940s and certainly in the 1950s.

Inside his truck was an assortment of staples that a farm family might need to purchase. Such things as bread, flour, sugar, canned goods, candy bars.

The huckster might have had a huge assortment of things. Frankly, I can't remember. Details have either slipped out of my head or hidden themselves behind more recent memories as I've aged.

I can't recall many details of the huckster or much else from those years. I think he came through only once a week, but it could have been more often. He stopped in the road in front of the various houses and customers – usually the farmer's wife because the farmer was out working in the fields – would walk to his truck and buy what the farm didn't produce.

The one detail I can remember is that he sold candy bars. In the hot summers of Ballard County, a Hershey bar bought from the huckster was always melted. There were no air-conditioned trucks in those days.

I've enlisted a couple of other folks to give me some additional information about the huckster.

My cousin Barbie, daughter of Herman and Pod, says one of the hucksters was Leonard Grief. "He had all kinds of things. I mainly remember the candy bars, but mother bought lot of things from him. His truck was kind of like a motor home and he had shelves in the back with the stuff on them. That is about all I can remember."

David Reid, who was a classmate and a basketball teammate at Ballard Memorial High School, grew up in the area. He remembered more things.

"One of the hucksters was Bobby Thompson from Ragland. Leonard Grief was from Ingleside. Thompson and his wife ran a grocery store in Ragland and he had the 'rolling store' that came by once a week," David recalls.

"When I was small, my mom would swap eggs and sometimes chickens for different staples. For me that meant an RC Cola and some kind of candy bar that was still firm, like a Payday.

"The big box truck he drove had cages on the back for the chickens he bought and sold on his weekly runs. It was a big deal for the kids because it was the only time they enjoyed such unhealthy luxuries.

"You may remember (name omitted to protect the injured). She boarded the huckster with high heels (the steps were grated to help keep mud out); anyway she got her heels caught in the grates, lost her balance, fell backwards and broke both of her legs.

"It's refreshing to remember in those days we were all friends and neighbors and you wouldn't 'sue' 'cause Sue was usually a girl down the road.

"Our dog loved to chase the hucksters; seems he thought they were chicken thieves."

I vaguely remember that most of the merchandise in the huckster's truck had a good coating of dust from driving up and down the backroads. But back in those days, a little dust, a few flies, even some mouse droppings in the corner weren't nearly the catastrophes they seem to be today.

Life was quite a bit simpler then, and folks accepted what came.

My cousin Robert Crice says this about the hucksters: "Regarding huckster – we called them 'huckster wagon' and I suspect the term goes back to the days they were literally a wagon drawn by horses. In any case we 'shopped' out of one in the early '40s. I started taking photos before the age of 12 while still on the farm where I was born. One of the photos was of Ralph Stevens' wagon that came to our area. The cloth feed sacks, with all their color, was one of my strong memories of the time."

Henrietta Smith Ross, one of my classmates at Ballard Memorial High School, adds these comments: "I remember the huckster as well, as I visited my grandparents often and lived with them during the first, second and third grade before I moved with my Dad to Florida but then came back to finish up my senior year at Ballard and stayed with them. My heart was always in Kentucky. I will never forget the pleasant odor of Leonard Grief's huckster and the dust. But I thought it was the most wonderful store there was outside of Bandana, that we didn't get to very often. I always bought the peanut butter logs, with the fuzz on the outside, because it didn't melt; I would hide them in my room and ration myself until he came again so I wouldn't run out. My grandmother, Grace Smith, married to Urb Smith, would sell eggs and cream and make purchases with that money. Guess there was some kind of refrigerator on board to preserve it or maybe not. Anyway, I'm sure the 'rolling store' couldn't have held that much stuff but my eyes were large at all the groceries and things to buy. I was always excited to see Leonard drive up to our back door and honk the horn. I was always the first one outside to investigate the goodies. I will never forget the smell and remember it to this day."

Liz Wolfe Miller writes: "Boy, does this bring back memories! Remember the candy cigarettes you could buy? We were so cool puffing on those sugar sticks with the dyed red ends."

Bill Wolfe adds this: "I'll always remember the Huckster Truck. It was hard to me to understand in later years why the word 'huckster' had a bad connotation, and was used to refer to someone selling overpriced, shoddy or fraudulent merchandise. To me, the Huckster must be a wonderful person to bring all those sweet treats. In my childhood, a nickel was plenty to buy a large chocolate candy bar or other snack, and Mother or Daddy would always give Liz and me a nickel apiece for the truck. One morning, Mother didn't have a nickel and she gave me a dime. A dime was considerably smaller than a nickel, so I felt terribly cheated. I wanted a big nickel and she gave me that miserly little dime. I cried and cried. But my tears dried up when they showed me how a dime could actually buy twice as much. It was a valuable lesson in the world of high finance."

The grocery store at Needmore

(David Reid grew up near Monkey's Eyebrow. He attended the elementary school at Bandana, a

few miles down the road, and he and I were classmates for four years at Ballard Memorial High School. He tells about the store at Needmore, a community a little east of Monkey's Eyebrow and the site of the Providence Baptist Church where Pod and Herman attended regularly. I went there too when I visited in the summers. Herman was the song leader. David submitted this story.)

Louis Berger was the proprietor of the one and only grocery store in Needmore. The other "business" was the Providence Baptist Church 300 yards due east. Mr. Berger was a recluse of sorts and not much was known or told about the old gentleman. He was small and frail and somewhere in his 80s.

He did not stock much due to a severe lack of customers. It was weird the way he sold his stock. He had his own method of rationing. If he had two loaves of bread, he would sell a customer only one with the reasoning that someone else might come in to buy a loaf and he would be out.

If you bought a candy bar (just one at a time) it was always wise to check it for extra protein before eating it as you might ingest more than you desired.

Oats, meal and flour were usually premixed as they had a mixing party of critters that came with the product. Strange how those little critters could get into things. They never seemed to eat that much.

Mr. Berger used an old mule and a wooden sled for transportation. When I was 12 years old I made the mistake of trying to pass Mr. Berger and his mule on my new 26-inch Schwinn bicycle. Mr. Berger was standing up on the sled as there was no seat.

When I attempted to pass the old mule it scared him so bad (guess he was daydreaming) that he lurched into high gear. He headed straight for Providence Baptist Cemetery at breakneck speed with Mr. Berger hanging on for dear life. They rounded the front of the church in a big cloud of dust with gravel flying everywhere and then all Hell broke loose. The sled caught on a big tombstone, the mule went head over heels and Mr. Berger disappeared over the top of a tombstone. I thought he had surely met his maker.

But Mr. Berger was sure agile for his age. He and the mule were both on their feet at the same time but the mule took off again before the old gentleman could reboard.

That was about the time I realized Mr. Berger must surely be dabbling in witchcraft or voodoo because he was sure muttering some kind of spell on me. The old mule was headed the same direction I was but he had a headstart and I was determined to leave the scene faster than he did before I inherited a curse Ajax couldn't handle.

I don't think I ever saw either of them after that. Mr. Berger may still be trying to catch the mule. If he is I imagine the sled is probably worn out by now.

The mule may have been eating the oats with the extra protein 'cause he was shore feeling his oats that day.

Anyway after looking around Needmore, it was evident how it got its name: It sure needed more ... and that was before the store fell in.

The physics of manure distribution

(This article was submitted by Keith Moss. Keith is the son of Joe and Barbara Tilley Moss and the grandson of Herman and Pod Tilley. Barbie is my first cousin, so that makes Keith my ... hmm, I never was able to calculate anything below first cousin ... let's see, that makes him my second cousin or my brother-in-law or my uncle.)

I remember an important lesson learned about mechanics and physics that I probably would have never truly realized in a classroom setting, but fully grasped while spending time at Granddad's farm at Monkey's Eyebrow one summer.

My Granddad and Grandmother were dairymen (probably should be referred to as dairypersons to keep with the PC crowd), and I don't exactly remember what time they got up in the morning to start the milking, but I know at some point I was awakened by Grandmother and sent to help with what I could at the milk barn.

I would normally shovel feed into the troughs for the cows coming in, and then help clean the milk barn and the parlor after the milking was finished. Once the cleaning was finished we would head up to the house to have breakfast and plan what else needed to be done that day.

With cows comes manure, and just outside between the parlor and milk barn was the pile. When we cleaned up after the cows, we piled the manure until such time that it needed to be removed. I guess it would be more accurate to describe it as being relocated to various locations around the farm to fertilize whatever needed to be fertilized.

We pulled the old Oliver 66 Row Crop tractor around to start the relocating process. We hooked the manure spreader to the tractor and parked them next to the large pile of manure and started loading the spreader.

After we filled the spreader, which looked like a three-sided wagon with a bunch of paddles and spikes across the back of the wagon, we would drive it out to one of the fields, move the long levers on the front of the spreader and then drive around until it was emptied.

The various paddles and spikes on the rear of the spreader would turn ferociously as we drove around, attacking the mounds of manure as they inched toward the back of the spreader, tossing it across the field leaving an easy-to-follow trail.

Well, as I was a fairly energetic young man, but old enough to drive the tractor by myself (probably 12 years old or so), Granddad gave me some instructions to start removing the manure while he took care of some other jobs that needed to be done.

One of those instructions was what speed to run the tractor while unloading the manure. I believe the instructions were to keep it in low speed in third gear and – since the Oliver tractor didn't have a tachometer – about two/thirds throttle.

This speed worked okay during the first trip out to empty the spreader, but once I got going just wasn't fast enough. I kept inching the throttle up, feeling pretty confident in my abilities and knowledge of this particular task, but it wasn't moving quite as fast as I thought it should.

On the third load I decided if I sped up the process I could get finished quicker and move on to more exciting activities. Once I got to the field, I moved the shifter into the Hi-speed position, and moved it into what would be fifth gear and kept it at the two-thirds throttle position and started across the field.

Since the manure is moved toward the back by a chain drive, the first couple of minutes were uneventful during the trip. I did notice that since I was moving across the field at a significantly quicker pace, that the paddles and spikes on the rear of the spreader were spinning at an incredible pace (mechanics lesson #1 – since the spreader was "wheel" driven, faster speed means faster spin).

When the manure finally reached the spinning apparatus at the rear of the spreader, it was like an explosion occurred (physics lesson #1 – the distance manure will fly is directly proportional to the speed at which the tractor is going and the paddles are spinning).

It was actually landing almost 10 feet in front of the tractor. Needless to say the tractor and I were pretty well covered by the material we were trying to get rid of.

The trip back to the barn ended with a quick wash with the hose for the tractor and me, and a little grin from my Granddad after he reminded me about the speed the spreader needed to be pulled at. I had to wonder as I emptied the last load if he had learned about physics the same way I did.

How many cars does it take for a traffic jam?

I was sitting with Pod and Herman in the front yard of the house at Monkey's Eyebrow several years ago, comfortable in a lawn chair, content with the quiet evening and an occasional comment.

It must have been in the late 1960s or early 1970s.

The road in front of their house had always been dirt or gravel. But after the state purchased much of the land in the river bottoms a couple of miles down the road, near Oscar, to create the Ballard County Wildlife Management Area a couple of years earlier, the road had been paved.

That was because people were driving there to see the beautiful scenery, the wildlife, and to hunt deer, ducks and geese during hunting seasons.

Anyway, we were enjoying the evening's peace and quiet when a car went down the road.

"This traffic has really gotten bad ever since they paved the road," Herman complained.

It was the second car in the last 30 or 45 minutes.

A couple of days at the farm

It's early morning, July 3, 2009, and I'm sitting at the kitchen bar in my farm home at Monkey's Eyebrow, gazing out the window at the cornfield, wishing an elephant would walk by. Not that I am particularly fond of pachyderms, and not that I expect to see one here near the western tip of Kentucky, but I'm curious to see if the corn is as high as an elephant's eye.

That might encourage me to burst into song.

Normally I wouldn't be tempted to burst into song. That would be grossly unfair to every hearing creature within range.

But … folks, there just ain't that many creatures within hearing range of my house. Mostly some crickets and other bugs outside, and

I did see a mouse dart across the floor last night. And now that I think about it, I don't care if they don't like my singing.

There are no livestock nearby that my singing would stampede, so I think it would be safe to butcher a few bars: "The corn is as high as an elephant's eye, and it looks like it's climbing clear up to the sky." But this is Kentucky, not Oklahoma, and let's face it, it's just too early in the morning to start singing about corn and various body parts of elephants.

My son Jesse and I drove down to spend a couple of nights at our home over the Fourth of July holiday period. The house isn't furnished, so we took a couple of air mattresses and sleeping pads and what not.

The air mattress is fairly comfortable but it's too close to the floor for an aging man. I put a four-time folded towel on the floor nearby so I can roll off the air mattress with my knees on the towel because the hardwood floor hurts if I'm kneeling on the bare wood, and there's a chair beside the towel so I can grab hold and use it as a brace until I manage to stand up.

If I'm lucky, I'll stand without losing balance and dropping back to my knees. Sigh. I can almost remember a time when I could have stood up without all the paraphernalia. Sigh some more. I can almost remember a time when I could have slept on the hardwood floor without any padding.

Anyway, here I sit, six in the morning, a little haze over the field, a little haze over my eyes, Jesse still asleep. Jesse doesn't realize that there is a six in the morning. He thinks the clock starts at noon.

I'm tempted to walk outside and take a leak behind the house or beside a shed. That's why men want to live in the country – so they can take a leak off the porch or in the backyard and to hell with the neighbors because there aren't any neighbors close enough to watch us without binoculars, and if they want to go to that much trouble to watch us take a leak on our own farm property, piss on them.

Besides, even if they have binoculars they can't see me over all that corn, which I'm pretty sure is at least as high as an elephant's eye, if not a giraffe's eye.

It was the first night Jesse has spent in the house. He was impressed by how quiet it is. Very little traffic, no noise except the insects. And he was impressed by how dark it is. When the sun goes down, the dark comes up and there are no street lights to punch light holes into the darkness.

Dark and quiet. A yard to take a leak in. Corn tall enough that only the top of the elephant's head would show.

If this ain't living, then I don't know what is.

Life is good at Monkey's Eyebrow

March 11, 2010

The spring peepers are peeping at Monkey's Eyebrow, I've put away the firewood, and I'm looking forward to planting a garden. It feels like spring. It's good to be settled in at home, especially now that it's getting warmer and I don't need to burn wood in the fireplace insert.

My farmhouse has an electric heat pump that keeps the house at whatever temperature is set on the thermostat, but there's something about burning wood that makes me feel more like I'm living authentic country style.

The crackle of hickory or oak giving up their heat is a comforting sound. And split firewood smells good, too.

I've found some bald eagles hanging around the Ballard County Wildlife Management Area just down the road from here, eagles who seem to enjoy having their picture taken. They sit patiently and unafraid while I snap off 40 or 50 shots. The bald eagle is a magnificent bird, but it has the coldest eyes you can imagine and some of the photos show that trait very well.

The spring frogs – I think maybe they're spring peepers but they buzz more than peep – are out in big numbers the past few days. It's good to sit out front and listen to them. Except for the occasional vehicle that passes by, they are one of the few daylight sounds. Birds are among the sounds, too, but the little frogs are more vocal right now. At night, we can go outside and listen to the coyotes howl. I don't especially like listening to coyotes so I usually just sit inside on my recliner and doze off until it's time to go to bed.

It's so quiet here. I heard the wind blowing last night but that just put me to sleep quicker.

I haven't recently seen the skunk that was living under the house. Maybe it got tired of sharing space with people walking above it and it moved out. I'll give it credit: It never sprayed us.

A couple from Paducah stopped at the house yesterday because of the sign in my yard: "Joe's Place Monkey's Eyebrow." The man had brought his wife to see Monkey's Eyebrow and they were about to give up on finding it before he saw my sign. It's hard to know you're in Monkey's Eyebrow. That's one reason I put up the sign. The other reason is so people who want to come here to buy a Monkey's Eyebrow coffee mug, T-shirt or cap will know that they're at the right place. In fact, the couple who stopped here yesterday wound up buying a mug and two shirts.

Well, I just looked out the window and I see that the sun is setting. I'll be getting sleepy soon, so I'll wrap this one up.

Anytime you're down Monkey's Eyebrow way I hope you'll stop by to chat. You'll know you're here by the sign in the yard.

Gotta go string some war

March 20, 2010

To paraphrase Mel Brooks in the movie Blazing Saddles, or perhap's this is a direct quote, "Work, work, work. Work, work, work. Work, work, work."

That pretty well sums up life at my little farm in Monkey's Eyebrow, Ky. Well, okay, I'll be honest: A lot of it is watching other people work. But I've been a whole lot more active since I moved here than I have in several years.

If there's this much effort involved in routine chores around a six-acre farm, how hard must it be to run a real farm like my son-in-law who farms around 2,500 acres?

Maybe not all that much harder, now that I think about it. The real farmers have tractors and plows and combines and other big toys ... er, make that tools, yeah, that's right ... other big tools to reduce the physical effort involved.

Anyway, I'm going out this morning after I finish writing this and string a little war. That rhymes with far, which is what you get when you strike a match. It also rhymes with tar, which sometimes goes flat on a car. And a farm can be a place where you grow stuff, or a handgun.

You may spell them differently and even pronounce them with the "i" that appears in their correct spelling – wire, fire, tire, firearm – but we hard-working farmers sometimes say them like I wrote them in the paragraph above.

Now don't go calling us uneducated or dumb or hicks or anything just because we may use alternative pronunciations.

I read somewhere about East Tennessee dialect, which isn't far from the way some folks talk around here, that it's a holdover from Elizabethan English. Then I read later that whoever made that claim was wrong.

I don't pretend to know the origin of some of our alternative pronunciations, but they work just fine.

The wire that provides support for my grapes and blackberries has just about rusted away, so I bought some new wire yesterday and I plan to put it up this morning. I also bought some more grape plants and I intend to transplant some blackberry plants.

Billy Pippin came by yesterday morning with his tractor and disk, and he disked up a garden spot. It's not where I intended to plant, but he explained why the location would be better. I watched him disk. Watching is work, too.

He was going to plow it, too, but he said it was too wet so he will come back when it dries out a bit. Wait a minute. I heard an engine and looked out. Billy is out there this morning doing something.

I have more than a hundred tomato plants to put out, which is way more than I need but I have to experiment until I discover which types of heirloom tomatoes I like best. I also have some seed for squash, watermelon, cantaloupe, beans, and corn, and several onion bulbs.

My sons Jesse and Joe Ray are working hard. Joe Ray is trimming oak trees at the farm owned by his mother and his step-father, and Jesse is cutting up the wood into fireplace size logs which he's dumping in front of our barn. We'll split them later and stack them up for firewood. I have a splitting maul for that very purpose. I also have a chain saw for cutting the wood.

Joe Moss, husband of my cousin Barbara Lynn, brought a tiller over yesterday for me to use in my garden enterprise. He even showed me how to use it. I tried to talk him into demonstrating how to use it by tilling up the garden when Billy finishes plowing, but he said instruction was enough.

Trying to talk kinfolk into demonstrating proper use of tools is also work.

Well, I've wasted enough time writing and sipping coffee. I guess I should go outside and watch Billy work the soil. Ah, this farm work never ends!

All roads lead to Monkey's Eyebrow

April 2, 2011

You will probably find this hard to believe but there still are a few people who've never been to (or through) Monkey's Eyebrow. I was surprised earlier today when a couple of them pulled into my driveway.

I had taken Brooke, the Lab, outside so she could get a little exercise and do any of nature's business that might need doing. She and Dora, the beagle, were exploring the yard when I noticed a van slow down at the Joe's Place Monkey's Eyebrow sign in the front yard.

It contained two people. After a few seconds the driver pulled into my driveway. She was a woman, probably around my age, and she rolled down the window. "How did the place come by that name," she asked, and I told her two or three of the stories that try to answer that very question.

She asked some more questions, including whether or not I was the Joe of Joe's Place, and then asked if it would be all right if they took a photo of the sign. Because one of the reasons I put the sign there is so people could know that they're in Monkey's Eyebrow and take a picture to prove it if they so desire, I assured her it would be okay to take the picture.

When I saw her taking a photo of just the sign, I asked if they would like to have me take a picture of them at the sign, and they said they would. The man – her husband, I assume – got out of the van at that point and I took a photo of the two of them.

They said they would like to get a picture of me at the sign, and I agreed to pose. The man said maybe I could hold Dora. I declined because just

about an hour earlier, while Jesse and I were
fooling around with the tractor, Bella found an
old paintbrush in the shed and a container that
held oil. The oil had probably been drained from a
tractor when Herman Tilley was still alive and
living here. I imagine it was at least 20 years old.

Bella decided it was time to do a little painting
and her 3-year-old mind thought the oil was
paint. While our attention was distracted Bella
"painted" part of the shed wall, part of my
aluminum fishing boat, and part of Dora. I wasn't
in the mood to pick up an oily dog.

The people were from Nebraska. I asked how
they happened to be driving past Monkey's
Eyebrow and they said they were on their way
home from a trip to Mississippi. I pointed out that
Monkey's Eyebrow Road isn't on the direct path
from Mississippi to Nebraska. I think they were
just roaming around in a leisurely drive home.

I explained to them that the Ballard Wildlife
Management Area is just two miles down the
road and they would have a chance to see some
pretty scenery and maybe some wildlife, so when
they left that's where they were headed.

Two fewer people who haven't been to
Monkey's Eyebrow. Also, two more people who
have visited Ballard County.

I don't know if they stopped anywhere to eat or
buy gas or spend money on something else, but I
think this helps show how any of us might have a
chance to make a good impression on visitors. I
imagine when they get back to Nebraska they will

tell some other folks about having been to Monkey's Eyebrow, Kentucky, and the wildlife refuge. They may have gone on to Wickliffe to see the cross on Fort Jefferson Hill. They will mention all of those things. Some of their friends may wind up coming here, too. That kind of networking helps increase the number of visitors who come through our county.

There are things in the county that visitors could enjoy seeing. One of our best assets, however, is the outgoing friendliness of our people. I know I made a good impression on this couple from Nebraska, but no better than any of you would have made.

Ballard County folks are the best.

Peace and quiet at The Monkey

June 5, 2010

I enjoy the peace and quiet here at Monkey's Eyebrow. I enjoy it so much that I'll admit it's a good thing I'm retired. I stay so relaxed that I don't believe I could force myself to leave for work each day.

My favorite times are early in the morning and late in the afternoon before and after the heat of the day, when there's almost always a good breeze. I sit in a lawn chair or the swing, enjoy the breeze and listen to the birds.

We have three primary kinds of birds here. Brown ones, red ones and black ones. Okay, I can't tell one kind of bird from another. I wish my friend Rick Borchelt would visit. Rick is not only the best science communicator in the world, at least that part of the world that lies outside Monkey's Eyebrow, but he's also an expert on every species of bird.

I can see a bird sitting on a limb and not be able to tell you what kind of bird it is. Rick doesn't have to see the bird. He can hear it whistle, or chirp, or grunt, or fart or whatever noise it makes, or just see the leaves rustle and he can tell you what kind of bird it is, whether it's male or female, how old it is, and what it had for breakfast.

Most of the time it would be absolutely quiet here except for the birds.

I don't want to give the wrong impression. I don't want you to think there's nothing going on here. At busy times of the day sometimes as many as a car every four or five minutes will pass in front of the house. Busy times of the day are rare, however. They happen maybe once a week.

I remember one morning I was sitting in the yard and three cars in a row drove past. Well, maybe I should have said three vehicles. I can't remember what kind of vehicles they were but having observed the traffic here I would lay odds that at least one and maybe all three were pickup trucks.

I don't know why there were so many in a row. Maybe they got stuck behind some kind of large farm vehicle down the road a ways. I know it wasn't my farm vehicle. I have a tractor now, but I don't know how to drive it so I leave it in the shed where it doesn't disrupt my peace and quiet.

I've noticed something else now that I'm retired and living at Monkey's Eyebrow. It's not really important to me what day it is. Tuesday? Thursday? So what?

And the news isn't important either. Before I retired, my morning Internet routine included about five or six online news sites. Now, I try to avoid the news. I can't do anything about most of the situations that the reporters insist on sharing with us, and the news just depresses me or it angers me because it's some meaningless information about a celebrity I'll never meet and I wouldn't like her or him even if we did meet. Therefore, most of the news just isn't relevant to the peace and quiet of Monkey's Eyebrow.

You want to know what is relevant and important? Naps, that's what. And now that I think about it, I believe I'll quit writing and take one.

Bandana Day, getting older, wet dream

My friend Eddie – Edward Faye, prominent attorney in Bowling Green, Ky., for those among you who prefer more formal references – and I were talking a few days ago about how much we were looking forward to a particular local event, Bandana Day.

Eddie started chuckling.

"You can tell you're getting old when you get this excited about Bandana Day," he said.

And that may be true. After all, the big doin's at Bandana Day take place in what is probably about half a block in length. The festivities aren't designed to enflame passions so much as to make people feel comfortable, feel at home.

Partly the excitement for us is that we plan to be among the vendors. I'll be offering for sale a Bandana/Monkey's Eyebrow T-shirt featuring a graphic design that I commissioned an artist to produce. Eddie will be offering some genuine, hand-crafted jewelry from Bali.

Knowing how things tend to work out for us, we both probably will wind up losing money, but that doesn't diminish how much we're looking forward to being part of the day.

So we chuckled about how two aging men (I'll admit it, I'm a little older than he is) have so little going on that we're looking forward to a small-town festival a month in advance.

"Yes, we can sit there at our vendor's table, drink Metamucil and watch the folks walk by," I said to Eddie, and we both laughed.

"But," I went on, "that's not the real indicator of getting older. I'm at an age when if I have a wet dream, that means I'm having a spell of incontinence and I've pissed in the bed."

We both laughed at that one, and commiserated with each other over the inherent truth. Somewhere back in school someone should have taught a class in what to expect during the aging process, what aches and pains are likely, what body parts are likely to fall off or stop working, and how Bandana Day will become a highlight of the year.

3 STORIES FROM BALLARD COUNTY

I wish we had cassette tape recorders when I was growing up in Ballard County, Kentucky, and that I had been endowed with enough sense to use one to record stories that I heard. But I didn't have a recorder and I probably didn't have the sense to use it if I had one. Here are some stories, some involving me, from my growing up years.

The other side of the tracks (bottom side)

Dugan Shepherd was generally well thought of around Wickliffe. He had lots of friends.

His wife, Rosie, might have helped keep him mostly on the straight and narrow. She didn't put up with a lot of crap. Apparently she had a bit of a temper.

Someone said of Rosie, "If they ever name a hurricane after Dugan's wife, you'd better hit the tall timber."

Dugan's actual name was Wilbur Lee Shepherd. His face was not quite right. A relative said that was because he was kicked in the face by a horse or mule when he was young.

Another relative passed on that Dugan taught himself to cuss when he was a kid by tying a string to his big toe. Every time he yanked the string, he said a cuss word. I don't know if that's true or just family lore.

Dugan was an ironworker. He worked hard and, as is the case with most ironworkers, he had periods when he was between jobs. Ironworking is an undertaking that keeps its practitioners in good shape. Dugan was a strong man.

He occasionally would go across the Ohio River to Cairo, Ill., and go on a drinking binge, or as some of the men put it, "go on a tear."

These tears weren't just for a couple of hours.

Here's how one of Dugan's co-workers once described Dugan's most recent (at that time) escapade in Cairo: "They were planting corn under the Mile Bridge when he went over to Cairo, and they were picking it when he came back."

I can't vouch for the story that follows as far as whether it's true or not, but it's a good story to tell.

The story goes that Dugan went to Cairo on one of the tears and managed to put away considerable quantities of the hard stuff over a considerable quantity of days.

One night he decided it would be a good time to go home and, seeing as how he would be going home in the middle of the night, he decided he might as well walk.

For some reason he chose to walk across the railroad bridge that spans the Ohio River from Cairo to Kentucky, or from Kentucky to Cairo depending on which way you're going.

He had been walking for a while, long enough that he estimated he must be somewhere near the middle of the river which flowed far below him, when he heard an approaching train.

Not having been on a tear sufficiently long that he was willing to face a train head-on, Dugan managed to work his way through some openings and hang onto cross ties or supports or something beneath the bridge.

He hung on for dear life because he didn't think he would survive a fall from that bridge into the middle of the Ohio River.

Finally the train passed over, but Dugan was tiring and didn't have the strength to get back up on the track side of the bridge. He was worried that he might not be able to hang on for much longer, and he wasn't sure how he was going to get out of the predicament.

Finally, he could hold on no longer. He hoped for some miraculous rescue, but his grip was slipping. It slipped a little more with each passing second. He knew he was going to drop. He hoped for the best and probably said a prayer as he started falling. He fell … for maybe a second. As it turned out, he had walked nearly to the end of the bridge on the Kentucky side, so he had been hanging on for dear life just a couple of feet above the ground.

The story, as told, doesn't say what level of hurricane he encountered when he got home.

What's in a name, Nick?

Nicknames sometimes replace given names permanently and irrevocably. This might be true in big cities but I don't have any experience in big cities so I don't know. I do know it's true in small towns.

Growing up in Ballard County, Kentucky, kids came to know folks by their nicknames. I never knew the actual names of many of the people.

For instance, there were the Haynes brothers – Dreamy and Possum – who ran a garage in Wickliffe. They probably started around the time of the Model A Ford and they were good mechanics.

They had been at it so long that their skin pores and the lines in the skin of their forearms had a permanent tint of grease.

I sometimes wonder how they would have fared if they were confronted by one of today's cars, which requires a "mechanic" to be more of a computer technician.

Another interesting nickname around Wickliffe was one I heard variations of. They include "Shoo Cat," "Shoecat," and "Shoecap." I believe his last name was Phelps.

I'm not sure which of the variations is right. Different people swear by one or the other. "Shoo Cat" makes a kind of sense. I have no idea what a "Shoecat" would be, or, for that matter, a "Shoecap."

Clifford Garrett was always called Wart. I'm not sure why.

Tommy Ryan shares this story about Wart.

Tommy's dad, Bill Ryan, who ran the Standard Oil station in Wickliffe, weighed a healthy 230 pounds or so at the time of this story, and he sweated easily, often, and in large volume.

One very hot summer day Bill and Wart were going to Prairie Lake to fish for crappie.

Bill told Wart that he had forgotten to bring water and was already suffering from thirst.

Wart said, "Don't worry, Bill, I iced down a case of beer."

Bill said, "Wart, I had sooner drink horse piss, but I guess it will have to do."

At the end of that long, hot afternoon Wart was astonished. "Bill," he said, "I would hate to see how much you could drink if you DID like beer. You drank 18 cans of it."

Some of the other names around town were "Racehorse" Reeves, "Wormy" Davenport, "Sheepy" Dupoyster, "Pig" Stewart, "Handsome" Haygood, "Chicken" Brack, "Sugarfoot" Rollins.

Speaking of the Rollinses, of which there were several in Ballard County, another one who comes to mind is "Coondog" Jess Rollins.

Coondog was well known for being tight with his money.

Eddie Faye reminded me of this story about Coondog Jess Rollins.

Coondog was a friend of George Johnson, who managed Wickliffe's tourist attraction, the

Ancient Buried City which today is known as the
Wickliffe Mounds. He often came to the Buried
City to visit Mr. Johnson, and it was not unusual
to find him sitting on the shaded porch.

A tourist was sitting in one of the chairs on the
porch, and was talking to Coondog.

After a while the tourist decided he was thirsty
and needed a Coke. He asked Coondog if he would
like one too. Cokes cost twenty-five cents at the
time.

Coondog thought about it for a minute before
he told the tourist, "No, I don't think I would like
a Coke, but I will take the quarter."

Let's see, there were "Block" Morris, "Sorghum"
Sullivan, "Sug" (or "Shug") Sullivan, the Giles
brothers – "Cricket" and "Dodge," whose wife was
known as "Tick" Giles – "Hop" Hopkins (that one's
too obvious, isn't it), "Pap" Beardsley, and Pap's
brother "Moose" Beardsley.

Or how about Jewell Ray Morgan, better
known as "Puddin," "Beano" Wells, "Shorty"
Underwood, "Wobbles" Thomason, "Punchy"
Garrison, "Chipper" Kinsey and "Squirrel"
Warford.

And finally, from the maternal side of my
family, there was "Billy Bob" Crice, whose actual
name was Ernest Wells Crice. I'm not aware of
anyone ever calling him anything except Billy
Bob.

The legend of Crazy Betty

She lived down the Old Blandville Road. Cruel and insensitive as we kids were, we called her Crazy Betty. Maybe the grownups did too.

They say she had been jilted by a lover. He promised to come for her. Local lore had it that whenever a car drove past where she lived, she would walk down to the road and stand, waiting for him to pick her up. Sometimes she was already standing there when the car went by.

A few years later when a young Tanya Tucker recorded the song "Delta Dawn," the story reminded me of her.

One night, either I had guests or my sister Jeanne did. This had to be around 1959 or 1960, because I was driving.

I suppose we must have been telling stories. Probably some ghost stories. It was late enough that it was dark outside, a good time for telling scary stories.

Either Jeanne or I mentioned Betty, and how she stood by the road, apparently waiting, waiting. Our friends were skeptical. "Well, let's drive down there and you'll see for yourself," we challenged.

We loaded into the car and drove the mile or two to where she lived.

It was a spooky night. Fog rolled low across the ground. The trees seemed somehow ominous, threatening in the Ballard County darkness.

There was a very large tree near the road, beside the driveway that led up to her house atop a small hill. In the dark and the fog and the mood, it could have been a hanging tree from earlier, more violent days.

We drove past the tree and the driveway and no one was there.

We continued on the road past the house for a short distance until we found a good turnaround spot so we could drive home.

The skepticism had increased. Our friends were convinced we had made up the story.

When we came to the driveway on the way back, there she stood, near the tree, shrouded and blurred by the fog, waiting for ... well, waiting for whatever her compulsion was that caused her to wait.

It was a sudden, startling thing to see her. It was like a scene from an unsettling movie.

It scared the hell out of us.

There was no more skepticism that night. I don't think we told any more scary stories.

Bob Level: Wart witch from Bandana

Folks say that Bob Level was a wart witch. He could touch a wart and it would go away. Or sometimes he would just say the wart would go away and it would.

He was from Bandana, just down the road from Monkey's Eyebrow.

My mother, Jessie Lee Crice Culver,
remembers one time when she had warts on her
fingers. She saw Bob Level in Wickliffe. She said,
"Bob, I have all these warts on here and they hurt
at night."

They hurt even when she put her hands on a
pillow at night.

Level looked at the warts and said, "Oh, they'll
go away."

Mother said she looked down one day and they
were all gone.

Daddy said sometimes Level would touch the
warts, sometimes he wouldn't. "He was a wart
witch. He was the seventh son of a seventh son, I
guess. That's sometimes the way it works."

Mother mentioned one time when her father –
Robert Crice, who served as Ballard County jailer
– had a "big ol' thing" on his head. He went to Dr.
Russell, a doctor in Wickliffe and a legend in his
own right in the area, and wanted him to take it
off.

Dr. Russell asked if it was hurting him, and my
grandfather said it wasn't. Dr. Russell didn't
want to cut it off. Because it wasn't hurting, he
told granddaddy, "Just leave it alone. Don't mess
with it."

But granddaddy didn't like having it on his
head, so one day when he saw Bob Level he
mentioned it. "It'll go away," Level said. Sure
enough, it just went away, just disappeared.

"You'd sort of forget about the wart after talking to Bob and all of a sudden you reach up there and it's gone," mother said.

Daddy mentioned a man he worked with at Oak Ridge National Laboratory. "I had a wart on my thumb and it bothered me," daddy said. "I was complaining about it one day and he said, 'Here, I'll just buy that wart,' and he gave me a penny."

Daddy said he put the penny on a shelf on his work bench and, "believe it or not," at some later date that wart went away."

Teresa Morris Salonimer, daughter of Charles (Block) and Aileen Morris, says, "Pug Hammett was another one who could remove warts. I had one on my thumb and Daddy told me the next time Mr. Hammett came in to shop at Sunlane IGA have him touch it. I did (though I was a non-believer). The next week, the seed wart dried up and flaked off."

A bucket of water and a baloney sandwich

One of the best meals I ever ate was a soggy baloney sandwich about 30 years ago.

I was in law school at the University of Tennessee at the time. One of my best friends in law school was Lee White, who grew up in Elizabethton in upper East Tennessee's mountains.

Up there in Lee's mountains, a couple of drops of rain can cause flash floods. That's not what it's like in Ballard County where the Ohio runs into the Mississippi. Here, it takes lots of rain to raise the river level.

Lee and I started law school at the University of Tennessee at the same time. We both were hunters, his experience coming in the pursuit of whatever critters ran around the mountains, while mine was mostly with the game you would find in a river bottoms environment. Duck hunting was my favorite, and at that time I usually went back to Ballard County each winter for at least one duck hunt.

Lee had never been duck hunting, so I invited him to go.

We launched our 14-foot johnboat at the landing close to the old pottery in Wickliffe, Ky., just south of the confluence of the two mighty rivers.

It was in November, maybe around Thanksgiving, and it was one of those days duck hunters like to remember. It was raining fairly hard, the wind was gusting, the temperature was falling, and the boat was overloaded with Lee and me, guns, duck and goose decoys, hip boots, hunting clothes, a tent, and a big cooler full of food and soft drinks.

We headed downstream to a sandbar island that had some trees and grass growing on it. The outboard probably wasn't big enough for the load, but I was confident we would be okay.

By the time we got to the island, we were both wet and chilled, which made it important to get the tent pitched.

We fought the weather and the dropping temperatures and the sand and finally got the tent up. We were exhausted, far too tired to try to build a fire in such damp conditions, so we crawled into the tent and opened the cooler.

We mashed some soggy bread, baloney, sliced cheese and sand together into sandwiches.

We each took a bite and agreed it was the best food we'd ever tasted.

Meanwhile, as we tried to hunt, the rain continued, the temperature dropped some more, the wind was creating white cap waves in the river, and we weren't having a lot of luck. Ducks had enough sense not to be out. Apparently, we didn't.

We had pulled the boat onto the island when we arrived and tied it to a tree. When we woke up the next morning and the river had risen enough that our boat was floating, though still soundly tied to the tree, Lee began to rant about how I was trying to drown us. I tried to reason with him that it took a lot of water to cause the river to rise enough to cover the island, but he was frightened.

We agreed to return to land.

This time, we were going against the current. The waves were higher than our heads as we sat in the boat. The small outboard was struggling against the current. One wave swept over us as we slid into a trough and filled the boat with water.

Lee gripped the sides of the aluminum boat hard enough to leave finger impressions in the metal. "You're wanting to die and take me with you," he accused me.

I tried to reassure him that we were okay, even as both of us dipped water out of the boat to lighten the load enough that the motor would push us against the current. I wasn't all that sure either that we wouldn't sink.

I told Lee that if the boat did sink, we should each grab a couple of goose decoys for flotation.

To Lee's surprise, and maybe a little to mine, we did make it back.

As we loaded the boat onto the trailer, I said, "Lee when we get the boat loaded, let's drive into town to the restaurant. We'll park the truck and walk in. We'll be wet and cold, but they'll let us in because they serve lots of duck hunters. The waitress will seat us. When she comes back with the menu, I'll say, 'We don't need a menu. Just throw a bucket of water in our faces and bring us a baloney sandwich.' "

Billy Ed and I had Butts in common

Billy Ed Boyd and his brother, Bobby, were the sons of Clint and Georgia Mae Boyd. They lived a couple of miles down toward Mayfield on what was then Highway 440 but today is, I think, Highway 121. We lived near Wickliffe, Ky.

Bobby was older. Billy Ed was a little older than I, but not by much.

It was Billy Ed who showed me how to make my first chords on my first guitar, a Silvertone.

He also almost taught me how to tune it. I say "almost" because most notes sound about the same to me. I have the tinnest of tin ears, enough tin to roof a good sized barn.

He showed me how to pick a couple of bass licks, notably some that sounded a little like a Johnny Cash song.

I heard from Billy Ed recently by e-mail.

He wrote, "Bro, it almost brought tears to my eyes to read your commentary. I remember the great times we had, thought we were s....... in tall cotton."

I'm not sure what the s periods stand for. Probably "sitting."

He recalled, "My first guitar was a Silvertone, strings so far off the neck that I just about had to take two hands to play it."

His second guitar was a Harmony Monterey f hole with a little amp that had a four-inch speaker in it. "Wow! I raised a tobacco crop to buy it for 75 dollars."

The Harmony catapulted him into the music business. "I played at several little joints in Cairo (Illinois). My first job was at Pinkies on 28th Street."

Billy Ed has retired, claims it's the third time he's retired, and lives in Alabama.

Oh yes, about the title of this memory piece. Billy Ed mentioned that he bought that $75 Harmony guitar at the Ray Butts Music Store on Commercial Avenue in Cairo. That's the same place I bought my Rickenbacker guitar.

Butts invented a special type of guitar amplifier with a playback feature. Among his customers were Chet Atkins and Scotty Moore, who used the amp in all the songs he recorded with Elvis.

Charles Wesley Hargrove's song

It's not a song you hear often, but on those rare occasions when I happen to hear one of the classic country radio stations play "Skip A Rope," I think of Charles Wesley Hargrove.

I thought of him when I read his obituary in the Paducah Sun newspaper, which reported that Charles Wesley died on July 29, 2008.

According to the paper, he was retired from the Illinois Central Gulf Railroad, was of the Pentecostal faith, and was a member of the Fraternal Order of Eagles in Kevil.

That's not much to say about a man who was truly one of the characters who came from Wickliffe.

Charles Wesley was six or seven years older than I am, so we weren't close. I remember him mostly from Dixie League baseball and from his occasional appearance on the bandstand at Club 18 in Cairo.

He wasn't up there often; in fact, it was a rare occasion when he stood at the mike. His appearances always seemed to coincide with a few more beers than he probably should have drunk.

And when he eventually cajoled whatever band was playing to let him sing, it was always the same song. "Skip A Rope." I guess it had some special, deep meaning to him.

Skip a rope skip a rope, listen to the children while they play
Ain't it kinda funny what the kids all say, skip a rope.
Daddy hates mama, mama hates dad
Last night you should've heard the fight they had.
Gave little sister another bad dream, she woke us all up with a terrible scream.
Skip a rope skip a rope...

Tommy Ryan with some input from his brother Danny shared some other memories.

Charles Wesley Hargrove was truly a "character" of Wickliffe, Tommy says. He was born to a father named "Private" and a mother named "Brownie."

"During my college years on weekends and summers, I drank many beers with Charles Wesley, Tony Phillips, Joe Thomason, and some others either in Club 18 or around Mound City Landing," Tommy remembers.

"I remember listening to him strum tunes of the '50s and '60s on his guitar. Some would say I wasted time and money, but Charlie and so many wonderful Ballard Countians gave me a great education in dealing with people. He was a most interesting character."

Tommy adds, "When I was a very young kid in the 50s, there was much talk about two local young baseball star pitchers, Charles Wesley the righty and the younger George Lane the lefty. Charles Wesley hurt his pitching arm as a senior in high school. Most people say he hurt it when he pitched an entire Dixie League doubleheader solo for Wickliffe while also playing high school ball, but many years later he told me he tripped over first base and landed on his pitching shoulder that day."

According to Tommy, "Charles Wesley was most personable and well-liked by young and old in Wickliffe. He poked fun at everybody, talked a lot, but his conversation was nearly always about baseball, the U.K. Wildcats or songs. He was a talker but he always told you straight. His only sins were his cheerful but loud and profane voice and eventually a drinking problem that he avoided until the end of his first marriage. When he would see me (or Joe Thomason or any other baseball fan), he would greet us at the front part of Club 18, bending over like a pitcher getting the sign from the catcher, or hold up his beer bottle and say '40 degrees... perfect!' "

He ended his songs or anything humorous he said or did with a loud, infectious laugh along with his natural uninhibited manner that made people warm to him.

One final memory Tommy Ryan relates: "In the '60s we all tried to impersonate Clint Eastwood's

'Fistful of Dollars' character, even going so far as to smoke those disgusting short, powerful twisted little cigarettes at the Turf Club, but Charles Wesley was the star because he was tall and broad-shouldered and had the older rugged face look."

Hither and thither and slither

Everyone who grew up in Ballard County was very conscious of snakes.

Many a snake has met its demise at the sharp edge of a garden hoe, beneath the wheels of a car or tractor, or by gunshot. Today when we are more sensitive of the need to share our environment with all sorts of critters, that sensitivity doesn't apply equally to all the critters. Snakes are left off the list.

A Ballard County boy (long since grown up) decided to go fishing in Axe Lake, just outside of Barlow.

The young man had a snake phobia. He is reported to have told a biology teacher who insisted that he dissect a snake as part of the classwork, "Go ahead and flunk me. I'm not going to do it."

He had paddled his boat into the water of Axe Lake, in amongst all the cypress trees where the living and the fishing is easy. A snake had been dozing beneath one of the boat seats. The snake decided it was time to wake up and get its morning exercise.

The story as told to me didn't mention the kind of snake, but usually when you see a snake in the river bottoms, it's a cottonmouth moccasin, one of the two species of poisonous snakes that shared Ballard County with us. The other was the copperhead.

It was fairly common back in those days to carry a pistol – usually a .22 caliber – when we went fishing just in case we were attacked by a cottonmouth.

The young man saw the snake, went into panic mode, grabbed his pistol and started firing. The nature of a bullet is such that it will pass through a snake and continue through the bottom of a boat.

He paddled frantically and made it back to bank before the boat sank, but just barely.

Asked later why he shot all those times into the boat, he gave the rational answer, "Because there was a snake in it!"

"I understand that part of it," the inquisitor said, "but why did you shoot 14 times?"

"That's all the bullets I had," was the explanation.

Makes perfect sense to me.

Billy Bob's longest pitch

What may have been the most impressive game of pitch and catch in Ballard County history took place more than 60 years ago and consisted of only one pitch.

E.W. "Billy Bob" Crice, one of my mother's brothers, was doing the pitching. Bill Weaver was going to try to do the catching.

A small group gathered in front of the Rudd-Wear Drug Store on Wickliffe's main thoroughfare across from the Ballard County Courthouse to watch the goings-on.

Billy Bob recalls that spectators included Harry Shelton Lane, Archie Wear, V.P. Rudd, Will Shadoan, all of Wickliffe, and Alvin Fisher of Bardwell. There may have been others, but no one took roll on that day some 65 years ago and those are all the names Billy Bob can remember.

Billy Bob can't remember exactly when he made the throw. He thinks it was probably in May or June of 1946, which was his senior year at Wickliffe High School.

The courthouse figured prominently in Billy Bob's life. He had grown up in the Ballard County jail. His father, Robert Crice, was jailer for about 20 years. The Crice family had living quarters in the jail building. The jailer's job included duties as custodian of the courthouse. Billy Bob helped out and was a familiar figure in the various courthouse offices. Later, after his father died and Billy Bob's mother, Lannie Johnston Crice, served out the remainder of the term, Billy Bob was elected jailer and then was elected sheriff.

But before his political career got under way, Billy Bob was a better-than-average pitcher in the old Twin States League. He pitched submarine style, where the ball is delivered in a lower-than-sidearm motion from just above the ground. In one game against Metropolis, he struck out 20 batters.

He decided he would try to throw a baseball from in front of the drug store, high enough and far enough that the ball would pass over the courthouse dome.

Asked why he decided to do that, he recalled that Archie had been teasing him about believing that he was "the best kid player in town." Anyone who remembers Archie Wear knows how it must have irritated Billy Bob to face the merciless teasing that Wear was capable of.

Billy Bob says he got the idea of throwing a baseball over the courthouse dome from reading about Charles Evard "Gabby" Street, a professional catcher who caught a baseball dropped from the top of the Washington Monument, a distance of 555 feet. Street was unable to catch any of the first 12 balls. He finally caught the 13th. That was on Aug. 21, 1908.

In Ballard County there's no Washington Monument, but there is a courthouse. Billy Bob told Wear that he was going to throw a ball over the dome on top of the courthouse.

Archie told Billy Bob he didn't think he could throw a ball that high and far. Billy Bob said that he could, and that Bill Weaver could catch it.

Unknown to Wear and the others, Crice and Weaver had been practicing the toss and catch off and on for a few weeks, and Billy Bob was confident he could manage to clear the dome.

On the day of the event, with the small group watching, Weaver went behind the courthouse and positioned himself about where he thought the ball would drop if it cleared the courthouse.

Billy Bob focused on the top of the dome for a few seconds, took a hard windup, and threw the ball as hard as he could.

It rose up and up, and then dropped down and down, having cleared the top of the courthouse dome, and landed in Weaver's mitt.

That wasn't Billy Bob's only legendary toss.

A few years later, having heard in a discussion about George Washington throwing a silver dollar across the Potomac River, Billy Bob said he thought he could throw one across the Cumberland River. This was back in the days before the river was dammed to make Lake Barkley. He was egged on by a co-worker who said he would pay him $25 if he could.

Billy Bob remembers that a crew from the Army Corps of Engineers was in a boat on the far side of the Cumberland, watching for the dollar to splash into the water.

But there was no splash. Billy Bob gave a mighty submarine throw and the dollar sailed all the way across the Cumberland into the mud on the far side.

Reginald "Catfish" Jones, one of the Corps employees who was watching the throw, saw where the dollar hit and he retrieved it, so Billy Bob not only collected on the challenge, but he got the silver dollar.

Legging it

It took courage to show some leg in Ballard County back in 1957. That's why Larry's mother came to me. Or maybe it was idiocy instead of courage. I'm not sure which.

I can place the time as being that year because I know it was either after we had finished eighth grade or just after we started our freshman year at Ballard Memorial High School.

Larry Harding was one of my two or three best friends at the time. His father was the Rev. Joe Harding, pastor of the Baptist Church I attended.

I'm not sure when Bermuda shorts first burst upon the national scene but I know when they came to Ballard County. It was in 1957. They probably had been around for a long time by then; it took a while for us to hear about fashion trends.

Larry's mother took me aside one day for a serious talk. She wanted to get Larry some Bermuda shorts, but he wouldn't wear them unless I did too.

You may wonder why wearing shorts would be a big deal.

Teasing was an art form in Wickliffe, where we grew up, and throughout the county. We rural folks didn't have a lot of entertainment available to us. Teasing was an available entertainment.

Larry knew, as I did, that a boy walking the streets of Wickliffe while wearing a pair of those shorts was an open invitation to everyone to make some sort of teasing comment.

I imagine his mother approached me for one or more of several reasons. I was a native of the town, whereas Larry moved there when his dad was named pastor of the church; I was a member of the varsity basketball team at Wickliffe Elementary School, which gave me a little bit of standing in the town; I could handle a certain amount of teasing without being destroyed emotionally.

Larry and I got pairs of shorts, put them on, and walked around town.

I remember walking along the sidewalk around the courthouse, where the whittlers and tobacco spitters and story tellers sitting on benches gave us plenty of abuse: wolf whistles, cat calls, derogatory remarks about our bird legs.

It didn't last long. Soon, others were wearing the shorts. It just took someone to be first.

It probably seemed to be a bit daring at the time. Today, those shorts are pretty tame when you compare them to some of the things people wear in public.

How do I remember the year so well when I have trouble remembering much of anything from more than a week ago?

Because I wore the shorts to basketball tryouts, that's how. It was in 1957, my freshman year in high school. Everyone else trying out for the team wore regular basketball shorts, which were a lot shorter then than they are now.

I endured another round of merciless teasing from the basketball hopefuls before I got a pair of practice trunks.

I had the last laugh, though.

That was the last season that the Ballard Bombers (that was our team name) practiced and played at the Barlow gym. Ballard hadn't been in existence for very long at the time; prior to the creation of the county high school, each community had its own high school and its own basketball team.

The new school didn't have its own gym in the early years, so we used the Barlow gym.

Because of the limited facilities, the coaches couldn't keep a lot of players on hand.

That year, only two freshmen made the team. One was Zack Hodges; I was the other. I probably owed it to the Bermuda shorts.

It wasn't all that big a deal. We were allowed to practice and dress out for home games. We didn't get to travel to road games.

And we took a huge amount of hazing from the upper classmen on the team.

Life probably would have been easier if we had not earned one of the two freshman spots. But at least it was a good excuse to wear shorts for the next four years.

Leave it a little longer on the sides

I don't go to barber shops these days.

It's not that I have anything against barbers, it's just that it's hard to find a barber shop.

Now most hair-cutting places are staffed entirely by women who call themselves stylists or something, but not barbers.

I suppose a haircut by any other name itches just the same.

Reminds me of a couple of lines from the album featuring Lester "Roadhog" Moran and the Cadillac Cowboys, when Lester is talking about his friend and sponsor on WEAK radio, Burford, who runs a barber shop: "Everybody who comes to Burford's has a close shave," and "Come on down to Burford's if you want to get clipped." Those may not be exact quotes, but you get the picture.

So I go to the not-barbers and they all ask the same question:

"How do you want it cut?"

That question always puzzles me for a couple of seconds, but then I typically answer, "Just like it is but a little shorter."

I mean, what could they do if I said, "Well, leave it a little longer on the sides and trim every other hair on top."

It was different when I was going to school at Ballard Memorial High School. Rules required basketball players to have short hair.

The short-hair expert around Wickliffe was Horace Gill, who had a shop adjoining his house on Highway 286 going toward Paducah. His son, Byron, was a classmate.

Gill was a master at giving flat-top haircuts. A flat-top at Gill's was truly flat.

The half inch or so of hair remaining after a flat-top haircut droops flat against the scalp, of course, so Gill also kept a good stock of Butch Wax, a thick wax that would make hair stand up straight for just about an entire day, and probably could double as axle grease if anyone needed to grease an axle. For best results, apply just about the whole can.

I forget what it cost to get a haircut, but I think it was probably around 75 cents at Gill's.

Horace and his wife also dabbled in TV repair and sometimes received payment by check.

I remember one time he showed me a check, written by a local person and spelled phonetically, as would not be unusual in Ballard County. It was made out to "Horse Gill."

Sticking it to the horse's rider

A big stick can be an essential accessory for the novice equestrian who overdoes it the first time atop the horse.

It can be every bit as important as a saddle and bridle.

There was a point some years ago when I decided I needed a horse.

It was one of those spontaneous needs that often arise, with no particular thought or planning that would cause them to make sense.

During that period, I actually had four horses. One was a strawberry roan racking horse. Another was a plodding black horse. A third was a black Tennessee walking horse stallion that wasn't a good walker but had been trained to rack.

The other one was what I called my Indian pony. It was a small horse, probably what would be described as a paint, with big red splotches over a white background.

I was hanging around at the time with Bill Patterson, who had a custom slaughter house in Wickliffe. He also had a horse or two.

After I got the Indian pony, Bill and I decided to go riding. We decided we would go at night, and our ride would take us into the river bottoms. We rode through thickets, crossed streams, found a few trails. We rode just about all night.

You experienced riders know what happened.

I got saddle sore. Very saddle sore.

It was really painful. I was having to ride tiptoe in the stirrups to try to keep my rear end off the saddle.

We came to a place in the bottoms where some pecan trees grew, so we decided to take a break there. We ate a few of the pecans and relaxed on our own two feet instead of the saddle. Both of us were sore.

We put off leaving but eventually it was time to climb back aboard and return home.

"Bill," I said, "do you see that big stick lying over there?"

He looked and said he saw it.

"Would you go pick it up?" I asked him.

He wanted to know why I wanted him to get the stick.

"You're going to have to pick it up and beat me with it until I get back on this horse," I explained.

Marshal Marshall's years as Wickliffe police officer

He came to Wickliffe in 1936 in a barge from Mound City. He was Wickliffe's police officer for about 17 years. He was scraped by a bullet once and shot at another time. He jailed a millionaire. The county drunk came to his aid one time and used a crotch grip to force the bad guy to stop beating him. And the young people of Wickliffe trusted him and were a regular source of information that helped him do his job.

It would have been correct to call him Marshal Marshall.

Marshall Pennebaker was born in Charleston, Mo., 86 years ago. He served Wickliffe as city marshal from 1949 to 1954, and then again from 1956 to 1967.

He could have served without a break except he quit the job in 1954 on a matter of principle.

Pennebaker always ran the police business the way he thought it should be run. Then in 1954, when Buddy Bell was police commissioner, "There was a kid who stole a bicycle and Buddy was wanting the kid put in jail. He was only 16 years old and I argued against it. It got so heated I just went down to city council and told them I quit."

Pennebaker was first hired as Wickliffe marshal after he served in the Navy during World War II. He wound up in the military, he says, because during an assembly program at Wickliffe High School he heard Anita Faye Crice sing "God Bless America." He was so touched with patriotic zeal that he ran out and joined the Navy.

Except for the Navy, the marshal's job was Pennebaker's first real job.

Asked about the philosophy that he applied to the job, he said, "My philosophy was always give a kid a break and they always gave me a break. They were good to me and I was good to them."

He tells a couple of stories to illustrate the relationship he had with young people.

"I went home one night and I was laughing and told my wife, those kids think they've got me figured out. I was in Doke's bathroom (Doke's was a gas station) and I could hear the young people talking about me. One of them said, 'Well he's a pretty good fellow but let me tell you one thing right now. If he ever starts scratching that damn bald head, you'd better pay attention.' The one who said that was Joe Giles."

Pennebaker said there wasn't anything the young people wouldn't tell him. "I'll give you another story on that. One time Anderson Moss was county judge. That's when the county judge had power. There had been some break-ins in Ballard County. I had to go to Cairo to get this fellow out of jail on some misdemeanor and he told me if I'd get him out of jail, he'd give me the names of the people who were doing the break-ins. I told the sheriff the names of about 20 who had done them. When they were having their hearing there at night, Anderson Moss wanted to know who I got my information from. I said, 'That's none of your business, I ain't going to tell you.' He said, 'I'll put you in jail.' I said, 'Well that means you're going to have to put me in jail because I told him I would not tell and I will not.' Jack Hall was the jailer. I got over there and I was laughing all the time. I said, 'Jack I need to use your phone. I want to call Judge Stahr.' (Elvis Stahr was the circuit judge.) The judge said, 'Marshall what are you doing waking me up at this time of day?' I said, 'They're throwing me in jail.' He wanted to know what they were putting me in jail for. I told him what Judge Moss said and he said, 'Put him on the phone.' He asked him if he wanted to go to jail instead of me."

Pennebaker didn't go to jail.

The young people in Wickliffe may have cooperated with Pennebaker but they weren't angels. Pennebaker tells this story about some of the young folks. "Kenny Teeters, Tony Phillips and I believe Punchy Garrison (Harold Garrison, later to serve as Ballard County sheriff) were there. This was back when men first started wearing long hair. There was a hitchhiker in town. One of them said, 'That guy needs a haircut.' About 15 or 20 minutes later Mrs. Joyce

Carpenter called and said, 'There's been a kidnapping!' I knew just as well what had happened. They had gotten that boy, taken him to the cemetery, gotten a pair of mule scissors and was giving him a haircut."

Halloween several years ago was a time when you could count on the boys of Wickliffe to pull pranks. Fred Byassee's barber shop was an annual target. Some years the front of the shop would be littered with truckloads of empty cans.

"They did that because Fred would run them away from the front of his shop," Pennebaker says. "I guess I was a little lax on that. One year I went by and the boys were standing across the street in front of Mildred Swain's. I asked them why they hadn't dumped anything in front of the shop. They just pointed and I looked. There sat Fred Byassee in a barber chair with a shotgun across his lap."

Pennebaker doesn't think there are many differences between young people today and then. He doesn't think today's kids are meaner, but he does believe that drugs affect them.

One difference he sees is that "the police don't try to help 'em. They try to squeeze 'em."

He said he used to spend a lot of time in Cairo at the Mark Twain. "If there was something going on in Wickliffe or Ballard County as far as that's concerned, I guarantee you one of these kids would come to Cairo and tell me I'd better get back to Wickliffe. They wouldn't tell me what was going on, they'd just say get back to Wickliffe. I never asked them why, I'd just come to Wickliffe. There was one time when Punchy Garrison and Tony Phillips got my blackjacks – I was in St. Louis at a ball game – and they had a man in jail when I got back. They had made a citizens' arrest of a man on top of the building, trying to break in down at Urban Hughes store."

But the drugs make a difference, he believes. "I think the dope has a different effect on them than whiskey." He refers to the Wickliffe young people as "my boys" and says, "My boys drank beer. I knew they did. I told them they had to clean the beer cans up, not leave them on the street."

Drugs led to one odd incident when he was serving as marshal. "They called me down to the Ancient Buried City (now the Wickliffe Mounds) one night, said there was a man down there chasing hogs out of the road. I got there and there wasn't even no hogs in the road. He was calling soo-ey soo-ey and making strange noises. I just loaded him up and taken him to jail. What it was, he was on a handful of pills."

Pennebaker was in some dangerous situations. There was the time when he stopped a car at the Gulf station that was operated by Richard Parham, across the street from the Methodist Church. The car had been weaving when it came through town. "There were five of them in the car. Four of them stayed in the car, but there was this big fellow about 6-9 or 6-10. He said, 'We're going to fight.' I was young and full of vinegar, and I said, 'That suits me fine.' He started in and two of them got out of the car, pinned my hands behind me and took my gun. He cocked that gun and held it on me. He knocked the fire out of me. Here come John Moyers. He had a radiator hose, and he was whupping them with a radiator hose. Ned Robinson, the county drunk – that I'd arrested no telling how many times – came up behind the big man and grabbed him by the testicles." That ended the fight. "Robinson came to my rescue. He said, 'They can't do nobody from Wickliffe that way.'"

Pennebaker got shot across the side of his head in the scuffle. He was holding the man's arm to keep the gun pointed away, but one of the shots came close, scraping Pennebaker's head. It was only a surface wound.

When Pennebaker started, he started out at $75 a month, and was on call seven days a week. There was no overtime pay.

Wickliffe had its own jail then but the city council didn't want to use it unless absolutely necessary. "When I first come back and started, they done the right thing and they told me to try my best not to put anybody in jail but tell them to go home. That worked okay for a pretty good while and then it got where they were having so many break-ins ...." That was about the time the city council bought what Pennebaker believes was the area's first two-way radio for local officers. He also was "the first one to get one of those modern si-reens. I thought I was in hog heaven. But it would save your life. It was a si-reen and a PA system too. You could sit in your car like at night time and say, 'Get out of your car.' You didn't have to walk out and get beside that car."

Pennebaker remembers the time he put a millionaire in the jail. Fain White King was the owner and excavator of what was then known as the Ancient Buried City. The Kings also owned the Magnolia Manor in Cairo. In 1946, King and his wife, Blanche, donated the Ancient Buried City to the Western Baptist Hospital. George Johnson managed the site for the hospital for many years until he retired.

During the transition period, Pennebaker says, King and Johnson got into it. "I always tried to settle things, to talk things out," Pennebaker says, "but King told me how he'd killed two or three people in Mississippi and how mean he could get. He was carrying a concealed pistol that he had pulled on Johnson. I knew it was wrong but I thought, 'I'm going to give you a taste of the Wickliffe jail.' Old George Marshall (who lived beside the jail) was sitting there and saw us drive up, and he came out there in his wheel chair and was the tickledest old man you ever seen in your life. King got him a lawyer and he sued the city of Wickliffe. It went on for about a year. His lawyer was smart and he told King, 'You don't want to go to trial in Ballard County. They hate you and they'll hang you.' "

Police got by with a lot of things then that they couldn't get by with now. "Several things we used to do, you'd be hanging yourself now,"

Pennebaker says. "Lloyd Key or myself, or Bud Shepherd in Cairo or the people over in Mississippi County, we'd have somebody you thought had done the crime but you couldn't quite prove it. What you'd do, you'd clean up, put your suit on, you'd go in and tell him you were his attorney, see. At the end of it you'd advise him to plead guilty. They'd put you in the pen now for doing that."

Another story Pennebaker remembers involved home brew.

He says there were "two old colored women" – Ella and her sister in Wickliffe – and they made home brew.

"Earl Johnson was sheriff," Pennebaker recalls. "He come to me one time and talked about raiding Ella. I said, 'Earl are you sure you know what you're doing?' He said, 'I know what I'm doing!' All right, fine. I think he got about four or five cases of home brew. He took them to the court house. About a month later they started exploding. In the meantime Ella had gone to court to get that home brew back. How she got out of it completely, she wasn't selling home brew. She would sell you a barbecue sandwich and give you a home brew to drink. They couldn't get her."

Pennebaker hasn't been able to live in his house on Beech Grove road since the floodwaters came up this year. He had lived there for 36 years and water never got into it until this year.

He has been married to Martha Sue for 63 years. She has been mayor of Wickliffe since the last election.

Today, his hearing is fading and age is taking its toll, but his mind is still sharp and he's a good source of memories about times gone by in Wickliffe.

Who's the home team?

Perry must have had a first name, but I don't believe I ever heard anyone use it when I was growing up in Wickliffe, Ky. People just said "Perry" and everyone knew who it was.

His first name may have been William. William Perry.

I remember him as maybe not the brightest bulb but as an outgoing, friendly person who would talk with anyone.

He would walk up the street, stop in the stores, and have little conversations with the people who owned them.

He wore his pants high, not up to the armpits but somewhere between there and his waist. He smoked cigars.

Archie Wear and V.P. Rudd had the Rudd-Wear Drug Store. Archie was just Archie. Mr. Rudd usually was referred to with that honorific, Mister, in front of the Rudd.

Archie was a nice enough guy but he couldn't say a complete sentence without at least three cuss words. He wasn't really cussing anyone, that's just how he formed sentences.

George Lane reminded me of this story when we attended the Democratic Rally at Columbus-Belmont State Park. George was there with his wife, Lynn Lane, Ballard County Clerk.

It was one of the days when Perry stopped by the stores and made small talk.

He came into the Rudd-Wear Drug Store where Archie was behind the counter.

"Archie, who does Wickliffe play tonight?" Perry asked.

"Well goddamn, hell, shit, Perry," Archie said. He probably didn't know who Wickliffe was playing, so he tossed out something. "They're playing Notre Dame."

Perry mostly made conversation; he wasn't really a big sports fan. So he asked the logical question: "Here or there?"

4 URBAN HUGHES

Ballard County had a high percentage of "characters" when I was growing up. Most of the ones I knew were in Wickliffe. Urban Hughes was one of the folks about whom stories of legendary proportion were told, and he was near the top when it came to telling stories himself.

His father, Jesse Hughes, ran a dry goods store in Wickliffe and was also legendary in stories told about him. After Mr. Hughes died, Urban ran the store for a few years.

Hanging around for the Harvest Festival

One story told about Urban Hughes took place during the Harvest Festival, an annual fair-like celebration held at that time in downtown Wickliffe along the street right in front of the courthouse.

No country festival at that time deserved recognition unless it had a dunking machine. Most of you know about dunking machines. For those who don't, there's a large tank of water. A wide board is affixed to a backdrop, extending above the tank of water. There's a mechanism attached to the device which includes a round metal target.

Civic leaders, school principals, lawyers, those sorts of folks and other volunteers take turns sitting on the board, taunting the audience. For a

fee, you get to throw three softballs at the target.
If you hit it, it releases a catch, the seat falls and
the person drops into the tank of water.

It's probably more fun than it sounds. But
maybe not much more. At least, it's a good
fundraising activity for the sponsor.

According to the story, some tourists stopped in
Wickliffe during a Harvest Festival probably 50
years ago. They came into Urban's store and
asked what was going on that drew the big crowd
and provided the carnival atmosphere.

Urban reportedly told them, "Well, we're
having a hanging."

"Good lord!" one of the tourists exclaimed.
"Why are all these people here for a hanging?"

"We always have a big celebration in town
when we hang someone," Urban is said to have
told them.

"That's awful," the tourist said. "But what's
that big tank of water with the board sticking out
over it?"

"That's our gallows," legend has it that Urban
said. "We have the tank of water there because
we're a good Christian town and we always
baptize people when we hang them."

According to some folks, the story didn't end
there. Wickliffe officials got a call some time later.
It seems that the tourists left Wickliffe and
continued south. They stopped at the first town
where they saw a policeman and told him he'd
better check what's happening up at Wickliffe

because the whole town is out there celebrating because they're getting ready to hang someone.

Howl, howl the gang's all here

Danny and Tommy Ryan, sons of the late Bill Ryan of Wickliffe, both have mentioned to me a time when Urban Hughes came home and led the neighborhood dogs in a howl-fest.

Urban's son Tim Hughes sets the story straight.

"As I think about it, when Urban came home and howled at the dogs, this happened on more than one occasion," Tim recalls. "However the most significant event that I remember happened probably in the late 1950s."

Here's the story as Tim tells it:

The most vocal of the neighborhood dogs were the coon hounds. And from time to time, the hounds would serenade the neighborhood (without encouragement). And they would wake everyone – living or dead.

Now some of the dogs in the choir were 1) Old Joe which was Roy Kimsey's hound. Joe was a growly, somewhat ill-tempered hound with a voice range between two and three miles

2) Next door to me at the time was Harry Rollins. He had some kind of a dog. I think it was a short-haired poop eater ... very noisy with bad breath. Come to think of it that also applied to some of the neighbors.

3) Around the corner on 2nd street heading north was Martin Robertson's home and he had some kind of a hound that liked to howl.

4) Then across the street from Robertson was the coon hound icon of Wickliffe, Ky. – Coon Dog Jesse Rollins. And he had one or two hounds. I think they were the leaders of the choir.

Sometime around midnight, my father returned from the Prairie Lake Lodge, and for whatever reason, Urban thought it appropriate to engage the coon hound choir in an A Capella rendition of the Battle Hymn of the Republic.

So, perhaps guided by his primordial instincts, Urban cupped his hand, placed it to one side of his mouth and began to howl and yodel. All the neighborhood dogs awakened and chimed in (VERY LOUDLY). And then within seconds, the porch lights in the neighborhood illuminated, and the inside lights as well.

I could hear neighbors cursing, phones ringing and a few other irreverent comments. Urban laughed, stumbled into the house, mumbled something about the call of the wild and headed to bed. My mom said, "Urban, you did that just for damn meanness." To which Urban replied, "They started it."

Urban vs. the lumber company for a spell

For many years, the Waldschmidt Lumber Company was a fixture of Wickliffe. It was located on top of Fort Jefferson Hill, on the opposite side of the road and just past where the Fort Jefferson Memorial Cross stands today, providing a fantastic view of the confluence of the Ohio and Mississippi rivers.

Urban Hughes had made a purchase there. When he received his statement, he took offense because his name was misspelled. The statement was addressed to Eurbin Hughes, not Urban Hughes.

"I won't pay a bill addressed to someone else," Urban is said to have told the folks at Waldschmidt Lumber. "My name is Urban ... Urban ... not Er-u-bin. If you send it to me – Urban Hughes – then I'll pay it."

Next month, he received another statement. You guessed it. It was addressed to Eurbin Hughes. He decided to get revenge so when he wrote a check to send to Waldschmidt Lumber, he made it out to Wallshit Lumber Company.

My guess is that they cashed the check. Money spends the same no matter how it smells.

I Like Ike: An Urban Hughes story

Some stories about characters in small towns start out as factual accounts of actual events, told because they are funny and reflect well-known traits of the character. Many of these grow with each retelling, refined into mythical proportions with only a grain of the original truth remaining.

Others need no embellishing. I call these "whole-grain stories." I don't know for sure which category this one falls into. It could be whole-grain because folks who knew Urban Hughes would have had no reason to question the content.

Bill Ryan, who ran the Standard Oil gas station in Wickliffe, had a Chesapeake Bay retriever named Ike. Ike was a well-known resident of Wickliffe who hung around the gas station with the rest of the hangers-on. Once a day, Bill would tell him to go get the mail. Ike would walk to the post office, where someone would open the back door and hand him the mail, which he would deliver to Bill.

During duck season, you would more likely find Ike in the cabin on Prairie Lake, where he spent time with Danny Ryan and me, prepared to retrieve ducks if and when we dropped any into the decoys spread in front of the duck blind across the lake from the cabin.

Eventually the day came when Ike died.

Urban Hughes, who ran the store that his father ran for many years, was one of Ike's good friends. When Ike died, Urban decided to run a tribute in the local paper, the Advance-Yeoman.

It was printed with a properly somber black border, as befits an in-memoriam tribute to a good friend. It extolled Ike's many virtues – his loyalty, his friendliness, his willingness to do his work, his dependability. It told how much Ike would be missed by the entire community.

Tommy Ryan recently came across a copy of the tribute. It read:

IN MEMORIAM
He cared little for worldly possessions.
He cared less for power or prestige.
He was devoted to all who deserved his devotion,
Especially those who were nearest and dearest to him.

He disliked only one or two who had abused him,
And he never forgot their abuse, and never forgave.
He never spoke ill of anything or anybody.

He had good habits and set an example in decorum.
He only wanted to do one thing with his life
And that was to serve, and he did it well.
So long, "IKE," you will be missed.
Signed: A Friend

Meanwhile ... a human resident of Wickliffe died at about the same time. His name was Isaac, but he was called Ike. I'll not mention the last name so as to avoid embarrassment to either family.

His survivors saw the tribute in the newspaper and, since no last name was given – I'm not sure that Ike the Chesapeake Bay retriever had a last name – they assumed it was written for their dearly departed. Somehow they were able to learn who had placed the ad.

According to the story as it's told, and I can't vouch for the truth other than to acknowledge that it is consistent with other stories, they decided to take up a collection for their dearly departed Ike the non-dog.

"Oh Mr. Hughes," they supposedly said, "we saw your tribute to our beloved Ike in the paper. We didn't know you felt that way about our dear Ike. But after reading your words we decided to come to the store because we're sure you would want to make a donation to Ike's memory."

Unfortunately for them, Ike the human had written a bad check to Urban sometime earlier and had never made good on it. Urban didn't have much reason to admire that particular Ike, but didn't have the heart to go into a rant about it.

Urban excused himself, went to a cigar box he kept near the cash register, searched through it until he found the bad check from Ike, he of two legs instead of four. He brought that check to the front of the store, dropped it into the collection container the people had, and told them, "Here's my donation."

Reading the Word ... almost

Here's one of the stories Urban Hughes told, rather than one told about him. This comes courtesy of Urban's son Tim.

Tim points out that it won't be as funny in writing: "The story, as my father Urban told it, was very funny. But without my dad's words and voice inflections, the story in text form loses much of the humor. I don't know or remember the names of individuals involved. Perhaps it's just as well."

Here's the story, at least the words, as Urban would have told it.

"Way back when .... now this was from the old horse and buggy days. One of the small Baptist churches near Wickliffe could not afford to employ a full-time minister. So, there were a few lay-ministers who took up the slack.

"The lay minister of this particular Sunday could neither read nor write. This particular minister liked to speak a few passages from the Bible to open the service. In order to accomplish the reading of the Word, the minister would open and hold the Bible. A literate deacon would stand behind the minister at the pulpit, and read (silently) from the Bible and then whisper the passage of scripture into the minister's ear. The minister would then repeat the Bible verses aloud to the congregation (and I mean really loudly with voice tremolo).

"Dialog as follows ....

"Deacon whispers to minister: 'And the Lord loved the world.'

"Preacher loudly to the congregation: 'And the Lord loved the world.'

"Unfortunately at this point, the deacon could not see the next verse because the minister's hand had covered the Bible text.

"Deacon in a whisper, 'Please move your thumb.'

"Minister to the congregation: 'As it is written, the Lord has commanded, you have got to move your thumbs.'

"Deacon in a whisper: 'Preacher ... you stupid dolt, now you've played hell!'

"Minister to the congregation: 'As it is written, you all are stupid and have played hell and into the hands of the devil!'

"The deacon left the minister at the pulpit, and exited the church along with half the congregation."

Drinking and dining don't mix

Urban Hughes, Bill Ryan and several other older men of Wickliffe would go to Bill's cabin periodically to cook steaks or catfish and maybe have a drink or two.

They had a name for their group. They called it the LD Lodge. I'm somewhat constrained to explain that, but let me at least say that the L stood for limber, and the men explained that at their age, the limber status pretty much summed up where they were in life.

There was a table in the cabin, with one of those slick table cloths that had pictures of fruits and vegetables.

On this particular night, Urban had enjoyed a good dinner and a few drinks. He got drowsy and dozed off with his head on the table. He came awake a little later with one of those abrupt come awakes when you jerk up but remain somewhere between awake and asleep.

He grabbed a spoon or fork, and started trying to eat one of the vegetables pictured on the table cloth.

Urban listened to the game without a radio

Tim Hughes, son of Urban Hughes, who was one of Wickliffe's main characters, remembers this story about his father.

Tim said, "Since I was just now sitting in my house watching a baseball game, I am reminded of the following story, circa: springtime 1960-something."

Tim had just gotten home for the weekend from college and he happened to run into Ken Rudy Doke, who was his next door neighbor at the time.

"Ken came up to me and said he had a bit of a scare a few days earlier when he arrived at his house. He told me that he saw Urban in his car in front of our house. And Ken thought Urban may have had a heart attack," according to Tim.

The driver's side door of Urban's car was open. Urban had his left foot out of the car on the ground. The car window was down and Urban had his elbow resting on the window sill. He was slumped over with his head on the steering wheel.

Ken Rudy rushed over and said, "Mr. Hughes, are you OK?"

Urban raised his head and said, "Yes I'm fine .... just listening to the Cardinals' baseball game."

When Doke told Tim what Urban had said, Tim replied, "Ken, that car does not have a radio."

Urban's dad was quite a character too

Urban Hughes was one of Wickliffe's leading characters. His father, Jesse Hughes, may have been even more of a character. Most people called him Mr. Hughes, or referred to him as Jess Hughes.

Here are three stories I've heard about him. This first one about patent leather shoes I've heard from multiple sources.

Mr. Hughes had a dry goods store in Wickliffe back in days gone by when there was an active retail establishment in town. He sold lots of shoes.

A woman bought a pair of patent leather shoes from him. According to my father, those shoes were quite stylish back in the days when women wore long dresses. Daddy says it wasn't unusual for a woman to simply squat in the yard back then when she needed to urinate. The long skirt protected her modesty, but not necessarily her shoes.

Daddy said that you had to care for patent leather with some sort of lubricant or polish, and if you didn't, the leather would crack.

Well, this particular woman brought her shoes back to Mr. Hughes and complained because they had cracked.

The story goes that Mr. Hughes took the shoes over to the window, looked at them real closely in the light, turned them over from side to side, and finally burst out, "Why hell, hell! You pissed on them."

I heard this next one from Bill Ryan and maybe some other people, too.

Here's how Bill told the story.

"A deaf and dumb beggar (remember, this was back in the days when people weren't concerned about politically correct language), pencil seller or whatever he was, went into Mr. Hughes' store, trying to sell him something, some magazine or something.

"He laid down a card that said he was trying to get enough money to go through college.

"Mr. Hughes put it down on the counter and wrote on the back side, 'You should have stayed home!' "

"As the beggar turned to leave the store, Mr. Hughes yelled, 'Hey!' The beggar turned around and Mr. Hughes handed him the card."

Daddy told me this one related to outhouse logic. For those of you who don't know such things, outhouses were wooden buildings back in the days before indoor plumbing, and they served the same purpose as a commode. Today they're made of plastic and called port-a-potties or some such clever name.

Anyway, Mr. Hughes told daddy:

"When you build your new outhouse, don't put two holes in it because the women will go out to the outhouse and they'll sit and they'll talk and they'll shit and they'll talk and they can't get their housework done. Don't build but one hole, then they won't socialize out there. But it's handy to have a small hole at a lower level for the children because they'll have trouble trying to climb up on the bigger hole."

5 RED HARRINGTON

Red Harrington of Wickliffe was one of the regulars you would find at Bill Ryan's Standard Oil station. If you set up a hierarchy of characterness among the Wickliffe residents back in the 1950s when I was growing up there, Red would be in the top tier along with such other notables as Bill Ryan, Urban Hughes, Archie Wear and a few others.

Red coughed a lot. I heard people say he had TB, but Red's grandson, Rick Harrington, said it was emphysema, not TB, that ultimately killed him. "He always kept a can of tobacco and his pipe and OCB rolling papers handy which I'm sure didn't help his cause very much," Rick said.

If an asylum, the inmates ran it

"If they surrounded Wickliffe with walls, it would be an asylum," Red Harrington once said. And Red would have been one of the people who would have helped it deserve that status.

Bill Ryan always had plenty of stories about Red, few of which I remember.

One was about the time Red was coming back from Cairo after having purchased a pint or half-pint of whatever it was he was drinking. Often after a trip to Cairo, he would turn left off the highway onto the gravel road that led to Prairie

Lake in the river bottoms. He'd go down there, relax a little, have a nip or two.

When he started to turn left on this particular day, a semi truck roared around him from behind, nearly clipping Red's car. Unnerved by this close brush with certain death, Red was telling about it at Bill's station.

"Well Red, why didn't you give a turn signal?" the people there kidded him.

"Turn signal hell," he retorted. "I did give one. But if I had the sun and the moon hanging back there for signals, the sunuvabitch would have still tried to run over me!"

Red Harrington and the salty dog

Red Harrington's wife, Agnes, raised roses at their house, which I recall being on the right side of the road going up the hill toward the old Wickliffe School, just past what is now the Wickliffe City Park.

A neighborhood dog, or perhaps it was a stray, decided that the roses were his personal commode, and he started leaving doggy landmines in the roses.

Red built a wire cage to go around the flowers.

According to Danny Ryan, the way the story was told at his dad's gas station, "The dog worked his ass through the cage, planted one turd and then crossed it with another, making a perfect X."

Red couldn't tolerate that type of insult to his wife and her roses.

Because the cage wasn't a sufficient deterrent, Red loaded a shotgun shell with salt.

The next time the dog came around to sign his name with the X, Red took aim and shot the dog directly in the offending part of its anatomy.

Danny reports, "The dog hit ground in the middle of the street, took a right on Sixth, and was last seen dragging his ass in sand to cool it off."

How to avoid getting any ducks

Red Harrington and Bill Ryan were duck hunting one day in the blind across from Bill's cabin on Prairie Lake.

Bill – probably with the help of others – would put out a spread of decoys in front of the blind at the start of duck season and leave them there all season.

The day of this story was a clear, sunny day, which often was the condition that led to the greatest hunting success from that particular spot.

Red had one of the coughing attacks that seemed to go on and on without relief.

Bill told him, "Red, I don't know how we're ever going to get a duck in here with you coughing like that."

Red managed to find enough time between coughs to come back with one of his typical quick retorts, this one aimed at Bill's thick eyeglasses: "Yeah, and with the sun shining off your eyeglasses like carbide lights, I don't know how in the hell we can get a duck in here, either."

If any of you readers are too young or too sheltered to know about carbide lights, they were used by miners before battery-powered lights came along, and they also were a favorite of coon hunters. People wore them on hats made for that purpose.

They would put some pellets of calcium carbide into the tank and add a little water. That produces acetylene. The gas could be lighted, usually with a wheel sort of like you'd see on a cigarette lighter. It produced sparks and the gas "whoofed" into flame.

Red Harrington: Two splashes, both of them big

Chicken Brack was a Wickliffe resident of ample proportions. That's a polite way of saying that he was a big man, with an abundance of insulation to keep him warm in the winter. In other words, he was fat.

Red Harrington went on a duck hunt with Chicken Brack in a small – probably around 12-feet long – johnboat. I don't know who sat in the front and who in the back, but that doesn't really matter. The force of gravity applies to both ends.

Red was not a heavy man. Chicken was. The boat acted sort of like a balance scales. Gravity causes the heavier end to drop and the lighter end to rise. Red's end of the boat, therefore, was out of the water with Red essentially sitting in the air.

Chicken's end of the boat was low, which meant that Chicken was separated from the water by no more than a couple of inches.

I think you can visualize how the boat looked in the water. Well, at least partly in the water.

They hadn't been there long before a lone duck flew over. Chicken had right of first shot. He shot once, but missed. He also missed the second shot. By this time the duck was directly overhead and Chicken – he of the ample proportions – shot a third time, straight up.

One of Sir Isaac Newton's laws of motion goes something like this: If there is a force there also is an equal and opposite force. What this means is that if you shoot your shotgun straight up, there will be an equal force pushing straight down against your shoulder. Or something like that. It's been a while since I studied such things at Ballard Memorial High School.

The laws of force worked. When Chicken shot the third time, the force pushed his end of the boat into the water.

Red said, "After the boat went under, the next thing I saw of Chicken was from the ears up."

Another time, Red was among the group of people – read that, loafers – hanging around Bill Ryan's Standard Oil station in Wickliffe on this particular day. It was pretty much a regular thing for people to be there, trying to outdo each other in stories.

For some odd reason, probably for the same reasons that bathroom humor will never go away, on this day each one was trying to position himself as having had the worst case of constipation.

It now was Red's turn.

"I hadn't shit in more than a week," Red reported, "but I thought I'd try to force something out. I sat on the commode for quite a while. I groaned, I hunched over, I groaned some more. Finally a 'three-cornered possum turd' trickled into the water. It hit the water and splashed so much that I was wet up to my armpits."

I suppose they get dense as the constipation persists.

6 MR. JONES

Mr. Jones, who must have been born old, apparently never saw a bad day in his life. Anytime you would walk past his house in Wickliffe when I was growing up, he would say, "Fine day, boy." Didn't matter what the weather was, it always was a fine day.

His name was Robert Herman Jones but I never heard anyone call him anything other than Mr. Jones or sometimes Old Man Jones.

Can I borrow something, Mr. Jones?

Mr. Jones was quite hard of hearing. If anyone happened to say something mean to him, he didn't hear it and he would respond, "Ah boy, yeah, fine day." His hearing was responsible for one of the oft-repeated stories in Wickliffe.

A tourist wanted directions to nearby Barlow, Ky., and he had the good (?) fortune to see Mr. Jones standing nearby.

"Excuse me, sir," the tourist said. "Could you tell me how to get to Barlow?" (Barlow is a town a little north of Wickliffe.)

Mr. Jones didn't quite hear what the tourist asked.

"Borrow!" he said. "I ain't got nothin' you can borrow."

The tourist was patient.

"No, I didn't ask to borrow anything. I want to know how to get to Barlow."

"I'm tellin' you, I ain't got nothin' you can borrow," Mr. Jones replied more adamantly.

By now the tourist was getting less patient and he began to shout.

"No you old man! I don't want to borrow anything, I just want to know how to get to Barlow!"

The shouting got through.

"Ah, Barlow," Mr. Jones said, pointing north. "Just over the hill."

My friend Tommy Ryan, one of the sons of Bill Ryan who ran the Standard Oil station in Wickliffe, adds these comments: Joe, as you know, Mr. Jones frequented the service station, though generally for a bathroom trip and brief chat with anybody willing to talk.

I still can hear that unusual twangy accent as he crutched into the station. After dad would give Mr. Jones a friendly greeting, it was always the same "Hi, Bill, hi boy, hi dog (to Ike, our fine Chesapeake Bay retriever), fine day, ah, boy, yeah." He made Ike pretty uncomfortable walking with the crutch, but we loved to hear the "Hi, dog."

As he would leave, if we were pumping gas into a vehicle, he would always become interested if he saw an out-of-state license plate. One friendly smile from the customer and Mr. Jones would stop and ask him "How are the crops up there?" The customer would usually mumble an answer. One of dad's favorites was the reply by a very

serious Michigan man: "Crrrrrops? Chrrrrrist,
pops, I dunno!"

Aren't the police friendly?

Mr. Jones was behind the wheel of his vehicle
in Cairo, Ill. The Cairo police thought he was
driving too slow and they wanted to give him a
ticket.

He was poking along heading south on
Highway 51. The Cairo police had two cars with
flashing red lights at 28th Street, trying to get
him to stop, and one officer standing in the road
with his hand up.

Mr. Jones thought they were being mighty
friendly so he waved at the friendly officers and
kept going.

On down the road at 8th Street there were
three police cars with their lights flashing. Mr.
Jones waved at them again and kept going.

When he got to the Ohio River bridge, he had to
stop because the police had the bridge pretty well
blocked.

Mr. Jones didn't understand what the fuss was
all about.

"I didn't do nothin'," he said.

It was a long sermon

Mr. Jones usually attended services at the
Christian Church in Wickliffe more or less across
the street from his house, where the Rev. Bill

Morris preached. He sat up front every Sunday — middle row, second pew, left-hand side looking toward the pulpit, according to Teresa Morris Salonimer, a niece of Rev. Morris. Mr. Jones was hard of hearing. Some folks say if you ever heard his wife sing, you would know it was a blessing in disguise.

On this particular Sunday, Mr. Jones attended church at Morris Valley Christian Church where Rev. Morris also preached.

It was a long-winded sermon and Mr. Jones had pretty well reached his fill of being preached to.

He pulled out his watch, checked the time, and said loud enough for folks to hear, "Too damn long, too damn long."

Any unsaved at the revival?

Wickliffe's Baptists were having a revival. Mr. Jones attended the Christian Church but Mrs. Jones went over to the revival service on this night.

The next morning, Mr. Jones asked her if there was a good crowd. She said, "Yes Herman, they had a good crowd."

"Well," he asked, "was anyone there unsaved?"

"I don't know, Herman," she answered. "I didn't go around asking people if they were saved."

"Well, were they any Baptists there?" he continued.

"Well yes, there were Baptists there."

And he wrapped up the conversation: "Well then, if there were Baptists there, there were some unsaved there."

7 DEEP THOUGHTS AND NOSTALGIA

Here are several stories that aren't necessarily about any of the characters of Ballard County, unless I'm willing to include myself in that group. Many of these are about discussions I've had. Some relate to random thoughts. You'll also discover quite a bit of nostalgia within this group of stories. The older I get, the more time I spend waxing nostalgic.

Elvis never said "Think you very much"

Have we changed the way we pronounce some of the letters, has the toning down of regional accents produced new sounds (if y'all know the answer, please tell me), or is it just that dotage is playing evil games with my hearing?

I had to go to the bank the other day because I couldn't find my bank card. I think I probably left it in an ATM the night before. Is that another sign of slippage?

The very nice lady at the bank was efficient and soon handed me a new card. I thanked her, using an appropriately southern drawn-out long A sound: Thaaank you.

She responded not quite in kind. It sounded like she said, "Think you."

I realized when she said it that I've heard many other people express their appreciation by thinking me or whomever it was who did something to be thinked for. But on those other times I didn't make a note to remind me to write about it.

Maybe thinking people is a phenomenon of youngspeak, that destruction of language by our youth which started with those attractive-but-inarticulate young people in California who munch on kiwi fruits and mispronounce words. It grew virally into a pandemic fueled by text messages, the rules of which apparently require that no word be spelled completely or accurately.

But the bank lady was not a young person in the age range that we normally associate with young people. She was probably in her 30s or early 40s (still is, as a matter of fact, which makes we wonder why I used "was" in this sentence), but whatever her age and point of origin, I'm pretty sure she thinked me.

I'm thinkful that my hearing is getting worse so that I don't have to hear all the other pronunciation decline.

I also notice more people talking too fast. In Ballard County when we were growing up, people weren't so rushed that they couldn't take their time to say a sentence at a relaxing pace that didn't set the listener's nerves ajar.

There was no need to rush. We didn't have fax machines and cell phones and instant messages where everything has to be said and done right now. We could actually wait for a letter to be written at point A and be delivered to us days later at point B. We could give a few minutes for a peaceful sentence to be said.

Everything happens so immediately today that I guess people don't have time to talk.

More than once I've told someone, "Please slow down. You're speaking faster than I can hear."

What about a fortunate accident?

Yesterday (today being the day I'm writing this) I got a call on my cell phone. The screen said the caller's ID was unavailable. I don't dodge calls so I answered anyway.

Turns out the call was from a representative of a financial company with which I've done business. The caller read from a script. After the first sentence, it was obvious this person had intruded into my cell phone in order to sell me some type of insurance that would pay all my bills.

She was telling what it would do for me. She started a sentence, "If you should meet with an unfortunate accident, God forbid, this will ...."

I interrupted.

But first ... have you noticed that when anyone says "God forbid," he or she is trying to sell you something? It might be a product, or it might be merely a point of view. But it is a sales pitch.

"If 'something should happen to you,' God forbid ...." Two things stand out in that pitch. One is that the salesperson is avoiding the concept that you might die. "If something should happen to you" is avoidance talk for "When you die." Second, it's a sales pitch. "God forbid" always is a sales pitch.

Now, back to the story:

"But what happens if I meet with a fortunate accident?" I asked her.

"What do you mean?" she stammered.

"Well," I said, "you were about to tell me what I would get if I should have an unfortunate accident. I want to know if I also receive benefits if I have a fortunate accident."

"I don't understand what a 'fortunate' accident' is," she said.

"Well, I'm not sure I do either," I continued, "but you said that whatever you're trying to sell me applies to an 'unfortunate' accident, God forbid. When you use an adjective in that way, it's because you're singling out a particular type of event that's covered. That implies that the opposite kind of event might not be covered. For instance, if you offered insurance that covers 'natural death,' it would be reasonable for me to assume that it does not cover 'unnatural death.' Therefore, when you start out talking about an unfortunate accident, I can only conclude that the fine print contains exclusions so that if I should have a fortunate accident, you would try to get out of paying for anything.

"Now that I understand that you're trying to cheat me out of benefits before we even do business, I don't want to talk to you any longer."

And I hung up

How about a research grant for ME?

I worked in public affairs at two national laboratories. I retired as a federal employee at the Department of Energy's National Energy Technology Laboratory, whose main mission was to find ways to continue using fossil fuels without harming the environment.

I saw today that DOE's Office of Fossil Energy has started a new newsletter, named Fossil Energy Today. I thought it would be fun to do a little tongue-in-cheek correspondence with a friend at DOE, so I sent him this e-mail.

"I just looked at the new newsletter. You can imagine my disappointment when I saw no stories about Monkey's Eyebrow and the reserves of fossil fuels that don't exist here. I am hoping to get a hefty DOE grant to import and implant some fossil fuel resources into the underlying geological strata here. Unfortunately, most of those strata consist of water. But when it comes time to extract the oil we import, it should be easy to do because oil and water don't mix. Just skim off everything that isn't water.

"We probably don't need to implant any coal. There is (or at least was) plenty of that just up the road in Muhlenberg County. I think I heard somewhere, though, that Mr. Peabody's coal train hauled it away."

In the same spirit, my friend responded:

"How are you? Great to hear you are alive and well. You know, we were saying just the other day that the one thing we need is a foreign correspondent for the newsletter. While it isn't exactly London or Paris or Dubai, perhaps if you got that hefty grant for R&D you could serve as our Monkey's Eyebrow correspondent to let us know how you're spending the taxpayers' money."

To which I wrote:

"I like your idea except for one small issue. I really don't want to have to tell anyone how I'm spending the taxpayers' money that will be invested in this first-of-a-kind R&D project. I've researched this carefully and discovered that there has never been an energy-related R&D grant awarded to anyone in Monkey's Eyebrow.

"I'll be establishing the Monkey's Eyebrow Local and International Center for Advanced Studies and Research into the Feasibility of Exploring for Undiscovered and Nonexistent Fossil Energy Reserves beneath the Farm Land in the Vicinity of Monkey's Eyebrow, Kentucky, Located within Ballard County, Kentucky. That's a long name, which is why we go by our acronym: MELICASRFEUNFERBFLMEKLBCK. That's a long acronym, so certainly the government will love us. We usually don't try to write out all the letters, we just pronounce the acronym or, to make it even simpler, refer to it as ME. Please send the check to ME. I've got to run out and buy a bigger wheelbarrow that will hold the money you're giving ME. Thanks for confirming my grant."

My friend wrote back that he was rolling on the floor. I stopped writing at that point because anytime a federal employee starts having a fit like that, I leave him alone until he recovers.

Paranoia in the public privy

Like so many others who have problems, I'm going to blame mine on the news media. It's not so much what they wrote or announced; in fact, it's their fault because they didn't give the complete story.

This goes back a few years to when Sen. Larry Craig got into trouble because – a policeman says – he was making secret signs in a public restroom at an airport.

Uh oh, I feel a quick diversion coming on. I can't imagine how it must feel to make your living as a law enforcement officer forced to hang out in public restrooms, looking and listening for secret messages from senators. The stakeout is bad enough; what's just as bad or even worse is being forced to learn all the secret codes. Unless you already know them.

Innocent me, I didn't know there were codes people use in restrooms to entice other people – but only those who know the secret codes – into … well, a same-sex quickie in the restroom stall.

Back to the discussion.

Okay, so the news media told us that certain things send seductive messages beneath and through the stalls.

Tapping the foot is one. Putting your fingers beneath the stall and wiggling them seductively is another. Letting your size 13 shoe wander from your stall into an adjacent one also is code.

Okay, that's three.

But there must be more. News media people, why didn't you report the whole list?

I can't go into a public restroom today without worrying what I might be doing that is a secret code no one told me about.

Are there certain grunts and groans that signal willingness to share a groan with the person in the next stall?

What if I'm reading a magazine and lay it on the floor? Am I asking for attention that I don't want?

And are these codes limited to public restrooms, and just those at airports?

Is there another set of codes for bus stations?

Are there codes for other settings, such as a restaurant or a bar?

Let's say I'm at the salad bar and I say something like, "Those certainly are some juicy looking garbanzos." Am I inadvertently saying to the guy in front of or behind me, "Hey Bullethead Bob, would you like to fool around in the rutabaga patch?"

Or let's say I'm sitting in a bar, listening to the band. I tap my fingers against the bar in time to the music. Am I unwittingly saying to the guitar player, "How would you like to come up to my place and pluck a few strings?"

Are any of you old enough to remember the old Buster Brown Show in the early days of TV? I believe the host was Andy Devine. He would say at least once each show, "Plunk your magic twanger, Froggy."

I wasn't aware of secret sex signals back then … now that I admit it, I wasn't aware of much of anything back then … but having learned about toe tapping and other secret signals through the news accounts, I'm afraid to even guess what secret message was being relayed by "Plunk your magic twanger."

Someone owes it to us to compile a book, or at least a list, of secret signals that send messages of desire.

And whoever compiles it, be sure to explain the perversions behind "Plunk your magic twanger."

You'd butter try a glass, and a mess of catfish

It's surprising how many people don't appreciate a glass of good, cold buttermilk. Buttermilk may be a southern thing. I've noticed that folks from Up North don't seem to know what you're talking about if the conversation happens to turn to buttermilk.

Of course, conversations rarely turn to buttermilk. There are too many depressing things that folks seem to find more interesting. Hurricanes. Members of Congress. Sickness.

Forest fires. Floods. Something as joyful as buttermilk has to take a backseat in discussions.

I remember that my grandmother Edna Culver sometimes made buttermilk, but I can't remember how she did it. Anyway, it's a lot more convenient to buy it already made. I frequently get into a buttermilk mood and drink about a quart a day.

A couple of years ago when I worked at the National Energy Technology Laboratory in Morgantown, West Virginia, I rode the lab's shuttle from Morgantown to the site at Pittsburgh a couple of times a week.

The shuttle service consists of two vans. One leaves Morgantown, the other leaves Pittsburgh, and they meet roughly halfway between at a store, where the drivers swap vehicles.

On hot days, I often would go into the store on the afternoon trip back to Morgantown and get a quart of buttermilk to drink on the back half of the trip.

Ron Grubb, who drives the Morgantown leg of the shuttle, and I would have conversations extolling the virtues of various foods we had enjoyed. I often talked about the buttermilk, how good and refreshing it is, and what a treat it is to get some authentic, old fashioned, homemade cornbread, crumble it into a glass of buttermilk, and consume it.

A friend who was on the shuttle one day watched me drink my quart of buttermilk and listened as I extolled its virtues. It sounded so good that he said he was going to try some. I saw him a few days later and asked if he had tried it yet. The look he gave me was all the answer I needed. Obviously he had, and obviously he hadn't liked it.

I should have expected that. He's from Up North. Most folks from Up North turn up their noses if you talk about buttermilk. They turn them up even higher if you talk about an all-you-can-eat dinner of cornmeal-rolled fiddler catfish.

It's no wonder they had to attack the South back in the 1860s. They figured that any people who would eat a catfish didn't deserve to have a confederacy of their own.

Oh, and if you get into a discussion with one of those catfish-deprived folks from Up North, don't talk about eating fiddlers. They'll think you're into some kind of musical cannibalism.

Whatever you do, don't force them to try a mess of catfish with some sliced onion and white beans. They might find out how good they are and that would leave less for those of us who deserve to have them to ourselves.

You won't believe this but I swear that it's the truth. I've had some of those people tell me they wouldn't eat a fried catfish, but they have tried them baked or grilled.

That's disgusting. I think maybe it's in the Bible that catfish are supposed to be rolled in cornmeal and deep fried, preferably in a large cast-iron kettle if you've got one sitting around full of hot grease.

Anyone who would grill a catfish probably would put tartar sauce on it. Makes me sick just to think about it.

More on the joys of fine food

The story above this one is about the fine dining offered by catfish and buttermilk, not necessarily together because the proper etiquette of eating catfish calls for liberal doses of sweet tea. For those among you who don't understand Southern cuisine, sweet tea is iced tea with sugar added during the preparation, not after it has been brewed.

I was thinking about food this morning as I went to the grocery store and got the makings for rosemary cornbread as featured at the House of Blues. I encountered that type of cornbread on a trip to New Orleans where I ate at least two dinners every night. You can look up the recipe online.

It's nothing like my aunt Pod's sour cream cornbread. In fact, it's nothing like any real cornbread, but it's a good alternative, especially when you pour some maple syrup over it. Anything that you bake in a skillet lined with sugar is going to be good.

I made a big pot of chili last night. Nothing spectacular or unusual about it, but it was mighty fine. I used a couple of pounds of ground beef, two onions, a couple of large cans of kidney beans, one can of whole stewed tomatoes, one can of diced tomatoes with onion and garlic in them, a couple of cloves of garlic which I whopped with the cleaver I bought just for that purpose, a jalapeno pepper, a bell pepper, lots of chili powder, and some salt.

It must have been good because we ate the whole pot.

We also made sour cream cornbread which we baked in a cast iron skillet, which may be the only legitimate way to bake cornbread. The cornbread is gone, too.

People go to fancy restaurants and pay big money for meals when some of the finest eating is also some of the least expensive. A pot of white or pinto beans, seasoned with a ham hock, and a skillet of cornbead … it don't get no better than that.

Someday I would like to open a restaurant that features nothing but beans and cornbread. Instead of smoking and non-smoking sections, it will have farting and non-farting sections.

My cousin Jackie Faye, who grew up with our grandmother Lannie Crice at the Ballard County Jail and later in other houses when grandmother stopped being jailer, sent some thoughts on the subject of catfish, beans and buttermilk. Here's what she wrote from Florida, where she lives today:

"I probably told my grandmother at least once a week that when I get big, I'm never going to eat great northern beans, pinto beans, cornbread, or drink buttermilk. I'm going to have Coke and ice cream and 3 Musketeers candy bars every single day.

"Now we have those beans, onion and cornbread at least every two weeks and I bought a half gallon of buttermilk last week. I forgot how good it is when it is really cold.

"I can't get those fiddlers here. They only have those pond-raised catfish fillets.

"The only person I know at work who understands this food is a girl who has family in Poplar Bluff, Mo. She spent her summers there. Probably has more to do with the Delta than the South. Those carpetbaggers never understood the virtues of good food."

A ghost story: Noises, a head on the wall

Dick and Oma Dell Crice always said their house was haunted. There were sounds of footsteps, sounds of people coming through doors that were locked, and the shadow of a disembodied head that would go around the walls.

Dick was one of mother's brothers, and Oma Dell was his wife. Their son, George, and I were not just cousins but also very good friends when we were growing up.

They lived in a house on the north side of what the Wickliffe map says is Court Street, the street that leads up past the old Wickliffe School and on out Highway 121. Their house was just east of where you turn left onto North 8th Street. The next house going east belonged to Mr. Holt, and I can't remember his first name. There's a church there now.

I was reminded of the ghostly goings on several years ago during a conversation with Nola Garrett and Rosie Garrett, Oma Dell's mother and sister respectively, and George.

Legend has it that the shed behind the house was the scene of a murder some years before. A woman apparently became sufficiently irritated with her sister that she knocked her in the head with a block of coal and then chopped her head off, according to George. Adding authenticity to the tale, Rosie noted, "I think they still have the hatchet, or the ax or whatever it was, down there at the courthouse."

Nola Garrett, whom I always called Mrs. Garrett and so I might as well continue doing that, said that Oma Dell heard things there all the time. Actually, Mrs. Garrett said Oma Dell "heered" things, but I'll change the colloquial pronunciations into correct spelling.

According to Mrs. Garrett, there was one morning when Dick got up early and left to go hunting. Oma Dell dozed off to sleep again after he left.

When you went into the front door of the house, their bedroom was to the right. Immediately behind it was a screened-in porch with a door that opened to the back yard.

Oma Dell reported that she heard someone come in that back door and she said she thought the person was coming right into the room where she was. She thought maybe it was Dick returning to pick up something he forgot.

She waited for him to walk into the bedroom, but the footsteps just kept walking around and then turned and went back out. When she went out a little later, she saw that the door was still fastened, and then she thought, "Well, Dick hasn't been here." And then she got scared. Or "skeered" as it was pronounced by quite a few local folks, including Mrs. Garrett, back then.

Other times, Rosie said, they would see the shadow of a head going around the wall. "You couldn't see no body," Rosie remembered.

Dick and his brother-in-law Wart Garrett were out hunting one night when Rosie and Oma Dell saw the head, and when they came back, Rosie and Oma Dell had them go outside and walk around the window, "and there wasn't no possible way to throw a shadow in," Rosie continued. "One of them got down in the middle of the floor and crawled across it. Well, there was his head right around the wall. Whatever it was, it had to be inside."

The shadow that Rosie and Oma Dell saw had a nose and short hair.

The goings-on didn't run them out of the house. They lived there for several years and later moved to Cairo, Ill.

How about a few superstitions

I took a class in folklore at the University of Tennessee in 1977, the year before I entered the U.T. College of Law. The main assignment was to talk to people and compile various bits of folklore. It was an opportunity to come back home to Ballard County for a few days and talk to people I knew.

Here are some of the stores I compiled. These deal with superstitions. The first five came from a visit with Nola Garrett and her daughter Rosie, both of whom have died in the years since then.

A death in the family: Rosie started this one. "If a dog – a strange dog – comes to your house and howls," she said, "that means a death in your family. That happened. When we lived at Fort Jefferson, Lem ... a strange dog came there ...." Nola Garrett interrupted at this point, "Howled all night." Then Rosie picked the story back up, "...and it got in a path where Lem used to go feed the hogs. We had a path going up beside of our house and that dog got in that path and nobody'd ever seen the dog before, and he howled. They counted the times that he howled, didn't they? And Mrs. Garrett responds, "Yeah." Rosie continues, "And in that many days, Lem died. Now that was a fact. Then the dog just left and we never did see that dog no more."

Fatal ashes: Rosie recalled this one. "It's bad luck, you ain't supposed to take ashes out on New Year's Day. If you do, you'll take a death out of the house before the year's gone." Mrs. Garrett added, "That's what they say but I know there's been a lot of ashes took out that they hadn't been no death went out."

Hens or roosters: Here's another one Rosie remembered about New Year's Day. "Another old saying is, on New Year's Day, if you have chickens – Mam-ma and them used to have chickens – they say if a man comes to your house first your chickens will all be roosters and if a woman comes they'll all be pullets."

Hair and headaches: Rosie and Mrs. Garrett took turns on this one. Rosie: "You're not supposed to cut your hair in March, are you?" Mrs. Garrett: "You ain't supposed to but a lot of them does." Rosie: "They say if you do you'll have a headache all year." Mrs. Garrett: "But I don't think there's anything to that because I know lots of folks that's had their hair cut in March and they said they didn't have no headache."

Death or marriage: Rosie and Mrs. Garrett also combined to tell this one. Rosie: "What is it, that if you look into a cistern...? Some say that if you look into a cistern with a mirror and you see yourself, you're going to die." Mrs. Garrett elaborated on this one. "First day of May. Well, if you're going to die, why your coffin comes out in front, and if you're going to get married, why your husband walks out in front of you. You look down in a cistern through a mirror. There never was nothing to that. We've tried that out too many times when we was growing up. We never seen no coffin, never seen no man down there."

Harbinger of death: Here's an old superstition my father remembered. "If a whippoorwill lights on your front porch, or comes in your house, well there'll be someone in the family will die before the year's up."

The last word: How to leave them speechless

Sometimes it takes only one word to bring the discussion to a speechless halt.

This goes back to when I was director of public affairs at Oak Ridge National Laboratory in Tennessee.

A friend had been in the hospital for several days. The first time I saw him after he returned to work, I asked what condition he had.

He named some sort of abdominal illness, the name of which I can't remember, and said that his case was sufficiently serious that it could have been fatal.

Concerned, I asked, "What causes that?"

Jokingly and chucklingly, he replied in a pseudo-serious manner, "Well, Joe, it's caused by a large penis."

Not one to pass up such an opportunity, I immediately responded, "Whose?"

He was speechless. End of discussion.

Numbers are the enemy

I do all right with numbers, including such simple things as adding and subtracting. But don't get me wrong, I'm no mathemagician.

Did I hear you ask, "What's a mathemagician?" I thought it was a term I just now coined, but I did a Google search on it and learned it has been used to describe a number of people.

I'm using it to mean someone who's a wizard with mathematics. That person is not me. I'm not as bad as the hired hand who worked for one Kentucky gentleman farmer. The farmer was telling a friend how weak at math his helper was. "He has to take off his pants to count to 21," the farmer explained. That includes all his fingers, all his toes, and ... well, you figure it out.

I've forgotten just about all the algebra I learned at Ballard Memorial High School, but I can still say most of the multiplication tables, at least through six.

Driving the car the other day, I was struck by something of a mathematical revelation. That beats getting struck by another car or by a deer, of course, but is disconcerting nonetheless.

Here's what I realized: In the mathematical scheme of things, my age is closer to 70 than to 60.

It hurts worse to see it in writing than to think of it in some abstract way while driving. Now I wish I hadn't started writing this.

Look at that. 70. That looks like a lot. I'm not there yet, but having thought how much closer it is now than it was ... oh, say 50 years ago ... I can't get my mind off it. 70.

I'm certainly not alone in wondering how so many numbers latched onto me seemingly while my back was turned. All of you do it, too, especially after you pass a certain threshold. For some it's probably 40. For others it may be 50. Some may even ignore the vertical numerical accumulation until 60.

I've never thought much about it. Most of my birthdays, I'm not even aware it's a birthday until someone reminds me or one of my helpful relatives – mother, sister, child – calls to ruin my day and to gloat over the fact that I've gained one number on them.

I would like to attribute evil qualities to those who can't leave high enough alone, but the numbers speak for themselves whether or not a relative calls. The numbers are the enemy; the enemy is not he or she who calls to point out the number. That person is merely the evil messenger, a martial neutral somewhere between friend and foe.

I guess a better approach would be to celebrate the addition of one, instead of bemoaning the total. After all, many, many people left us sooner in their lives.

But I can't help it. It's like carving another notch into that path of inexorable pilgrimage toward the time when the plus sign goes away and the number gets no bigger.

Going nuts at Christmas

I was in a grocery about a month before Christmas and several bins of nuts caught my eye. There were Brazil nuts and hazelnuts, soft-shelled walnuts of the type we called English walnuts, pecans and other varieties.

Christmas seems to bring out the nuts among us.

It made me remember growing up at a time when, I assume, every family had one of those round wooden nutcracker bowls with tree bark on the outside and a round cracking block in the middle. The set came with a metal gadget you could use to crack nuts manually, and a set of some pointed picks for use in trying to pry the kernel out of the cracked shell. Maybe most people still have one of the sets.

Nuts were and apparently still are a staple at Christmas.

As I retreated into memory of Christmas nuts past, I also began to think about nuts and berries we outdoors types of people were familiar with.

There were lots of wild black walnut trees growing around Ballard County, and hickory trees and even pecan trees, especially down in the river bottoms.

I still think the black walnut and the hickory nut – or hickernut as we called it – are two of the best tasting nuts there are. Unfortunately, both are next to impossible to enjoy because the shells not only are very hard to crack, but they hold onto their kernels like super glue.

Walnuts also compound the difficulty by having that green outer part that surrounds the nut and is removed only at the risk of staining everything it touches. Walnut stain, like a diamond, seems to be forever.

I tried to cope with walnuts several years in a row. I tried putting them on our driveway and stomping them while wearing rubber hip boots. The result? Stained boots and stained driveway. I put an old tire on the ground and placed walnuts inside the part that would have fit around the rim, and jumped up and down on them to remove the green part. One misjump and you risk turning an ankle and falling. Out of bushels of walnuts, I might wind up with a couple of dozen de-greened.

After the exposed nut was dry, it was a major struggle to crack it open and pick out a few flakes of kernel. Tasted good, but maybe not worth the effort.

Hickernuts, I believe, were even worse. I never believed Eull Gibbons when he claimed that a cereal tasted like wild hickory nuts. How did he know? There's no way to reach the kernel of a hickernut.

Has anyone ever held an intact black walnut or hickernut kernel? Is there such a thing?

There are some foods I enjoy but have decided they aren't worth the trouble. Crab legs are one.

I've made a vow not to eat any seafood I have to beat with a hammer or crack with a pair of pliers. My theory is that there's a net loss of nourishment: The effort of eating requires more energy than is replaced by the meal. I'll take one of those Hardee's thickburgers instead.

Any of you ever try wild persimmons? They taste very good and you don't have to beat them with a stick or a hammer, but eat one before it's totally ripe and you wind up with a permanent pucker.

I was told as a youngster not to eat a persimmon until after the first frost. I'm not sure that even a frost depuckers a persimmon.

How about mulberries? Did you ever try them?

I think mulberries taste good but you have to examine them carefully because many harbor tiny bugs.

And you have to compete with birds for mulberries.

Birds like to fill up on them and then sit on a telephone line or tree limb right above your just-washed car so they can aim purple droppings that land every time on the roof or hood. Birds filled with mulberries are uncannily accurate.

A small dose of vengeance

My health insurance provider is Blue Cross Blue Shield. I had a very generic question that would apply to any covered person, so I called a customer service representative to ask how they define co-pay and co-insurance.

I told the customer service representative – or you can shorten that to customer service rep, and the rep or representative won't be offended – that my question was very general, not at all specific to any individual policyholder, including me.

I might as well have been talking to one of those hickory trees that grow in the Ballard County river bottoms, which we called hickernut trees when we hunted squirrels that gnawed on their nuts.

She went through the whole litany: My name, my policy ID number, my home address, my daytime telephone number (and that's one that always puzzles me because the telephone doesn't know if it's day or night), my social security number, the name and address of my first pet, how much weight I had gained in the past year, and the meaning of life. I got that last one right but I stumbled over some of the other answers.

And then I finally got to ask what they mean by the term "co-insurance" and she told me. The question and answer took less time than the interrogation.

I got a small measure of revenge today when the mail included an envelope that contained my new Sears card. The card had a sticker on it, demanding that I call the particular 800 number to activate. I called.

I went through the procedure. Push 1 for English. Push the numbers on the telephone that correspond to the numbers on the card. Push the numbers on the telephone that correspond to the three numbers on the back of the card.

It's been my experience with plastic cards that once those 19 numbers have been pushed, the recorded voice thanks me and says my card is now active. But today, the recording told me to stay on the line while I was transferred to a customer service rep or representative.

The first time, once the transfer process started all I heard was a high pitched squeal. The second time, I was connected to an almost-English-speaking person who claimed she couldn't hear me because of some background noise. She blamed it on my phone, but when I bought that phone I specified that it come background-noise-free, just to avoid such situations.

The third time, I was connected to someone who could hear me and whom I could understand.

She said I need to create a unique password, such as my high school or my pet's name and she asked for the name of my high school.

"You implied that I have options," I said, "but then you ask for the name of my school. Don't I have options?"

"You can use anything you want, like the name of your pet."

"I don't have a pet, but my mother has a maiden name. Can I use that?"

"Yes, you can use that."

I spelled it out for her.

I didn't say anything but there's really nothing unique about the name of my high school or the pet I don't have or my mother's maiden name. I didn't want to mention that because she might make me keep trying until I came up with something unique, maybe something like the parakeet I named Buzzard, and who died apparently trying to break out of its cage. I named it Buzzard to make it feel bigger and more powerful. I didn't know the name would be fatal.

So I gave my mother's maiden name, but I made it up to see if they would accept a false name if I ever needed to use my unique password.

She said they wanted that unique password so they'll know that they're talking to me.

"That's okay for you," I said, "but how I know that I'm talking to a Sears customer service rep? Do they have passwords that you can give to me?"

"No one has ever asked that question before," she said, probably just trying to make me feel important and unique, unlike the passwords she had tried to force on me. She pondered the question for a minute or two, or at least for five seconds, and said, "Well, you called us so you should know you're talking to a Sears person."

"Yeah, I called, but how do I know I dialed the right number or what if someone tapped your line?"

She was getting a little flustered. "We have caller ID so we can tell if the call is coming from your home phone."

"That shows you who I am, but that doesn't show me that I'm talking to Sears."

She admitted that I was right.

She said the password and the other stuff was to protect me from identity theft.

"Identity theft isn't a problem," I said. "No one has so little self respect as to claim to be me."

"But they might be trying to get your money!"

I laughed out loud at that, or, if we were doing text messages, I might say I l-ed ol. Does anyone say that?

I told her that some places ask for my social security number or just the last four digits.

"We will never ask for the full number, only the last four," she explained.

"Either way is fine because I don't give out my social security number, not even to the social security office, and that became a real problem when I tried to sign up for benefits."

I think that may have been when she hung up.

8 STORIES ABOUT FAMILY

Most of the stories in this book are about friends and characters from Ballard County. These stories are about members of my family, which includes my paternal Culver line and maternal Crice line. I'm very happy to be a part of both.

We got our kicks on Route 66

The most memorable trip I've ever taken was a few years ago – probably in 2002 or 2003 – when Eddie Faye and I drove along Route 66 from Chicago to Santa Fe.

Eddie and I grew up about a mile outside what was the biggest town in Ballard County at the time, Wickliffe, population 900. He was raised by his grandparents, Hub and Myrtle Copeland, two of the finest people who ever lived. They lived just up the Old Blandville Road from our house.

Eddie spent a lot of time visiting with my family because we were just about the only kids in the area. Eddie was like another brother, and he's more like that now that we're grown. Today, he's an attorney in Bowling Green.

Eddie called one day and said we should take some time off, rent a Corvette, and drive along as much of the old Route 66 as we could find. It was a good time for me. I was scheduled to attend a meeting in Santa Fe and was able to arrange to take some vacation time before the meeting. We decided to drive to Santa Fe and fly back from Albuquerque.

We met at the airport in Chicago, and went to the car rental place. They didn't have any Corvettes, but we agreed to take a Mustang which should provide nearly the same excitement as the guys used to have on the old TV series. We waited and waited for them to bring us the Mustang. Finally we went to the checkout counter and asked what was the holdup. "Oh, we don't have any Mustangs," we were told. Turned out, they never did have them, which made it strange that they had told us to wait while they brought us one.

We wound up in a Mercury Grand Marquis, not quite the same cool car we wanted but after a few days on the road we were happy we had the bigger, more comfortable auto.

We joked, laughed, reminisced and had terrific opportunities to talk with people along the way. We took lots of photos, ate lots of food, and had lots of fun. We drove through Illinois, Missouri, probably part of Arkansas, Kansas, Oklahoma, maybe Texas, New Mexico and I can't remember all of the states.

I believe we were spending this particular night in Joplin, Missouri. We went for dinner to a large barbecue place. The receptionist just inside the door was a buxom, beautiful young woman showing an adequate view of her cleavage.

"How many in your party?" she asked.

"Just the two of us," we answered. "We couldn't find anyone to have dinner with us."

"Aw, I can't believe that, not for a couple of studs like you," she said, clearly recognizing our studliness which we had not even been aware of before she brought it to our attention. If nothing else notable had happened the entire trip, we would have been floating above ground the rest of the way anyway, after having been acknowledged as a "couple of studs" by such an attractive woman.

We left a good tip.

Another overnight stop, perhaps in Oklahoma, and another dinner in a restaurant. The crowd had thinned out by the time we got there and our server – who was nowhere near as interesting visually as the receptionist in Joplin – seemed attracted to us, so she stopped by occasionally to talk.

When we told her we were driving Route 66 to Santa Fe, she said she had lived there once. "I used to be married to a preacher," she told us, "but I ran off with a younger man and we moved to Santa Fe. I had to leave eventually because he was abusing me and I didn't like some of the abuse." Neither Eddie nor I had the forwardness to ask her which abuse she did like.

We talked with people at restaurants, gas stations, tourist stops, and each conversation was a great experience. We felt like family with the folks who lived and worked along the parts of the highway that we traveled.

We didn't always stay on the highway. Eddie had bought some maps that showed where original parts of the Mother Road still remain. He pointed to one side road and said that it was a part of that original road. I was a little suspicious when we crossed over a cattle grate onto a dirt road where the ruts had grass growing on both sides and in the middle.

Suspicion grew when we drove through a herd of cattle, many of which stopped whatever they were doing and looked at us as if asking, "What are you doing out in this field?"

Sharp dropoffs on both sides of the road into deep chasms, more grass in the ruts, no sign of any buildings within a few miles and we were getting confident this wasn't part of the original Route 66. When the road ended at a barbed wire fence, just beyond which was the edge of the world, where it dropped off perpendicularly into a bottomless pit, we decided we'd better turn around and go back. The cattle were waiting there, expecting us. They knew we were lost.

The greatest memory of the trip was at the Albuquerque airport, where we had plane reservations to fly back. That was at a time when airport security was really strict. I think they opened every bag. The line snaked around and around, with what seemed like hundreds of people.

At one point, we allowed a group of folks to get in front of us. It was a young woman – very attractive, which probably is at least part of the reason we let them in – with five children. We talked with her and learned she was a social worker taking the Navaho brothers and sisters to relatives in Utah, removing them from an abusive situation at home.

My heart melted when the youngest girl, probably around three or four years old, looked up into my eyes and smiled at me. We invited them to join us for lunch, which we purchased, and then we took them to the airport gift shop and let each child pick out something, which we bought. Our generosity was made possible in part because each of us had won $400 or $500 the day before at slot machines at a Pueblo casino near Santa Fe.

We had such a good time with the children that it seemed almost like they were ours. Finally it was time for them to go to their gate and us to ours. Eddie and I both were shedding tears when they left.

We were sitting at our gate talking about how intense our feelings were for the children when we looked up and saw them coming toward us. The social worker – Jennifer was her name – said she had never had anything like this happen before. When they were walking toward their gate, the children all said they wanted to come back and say goodbye to Eddie and Joe again.

I probably don't have to report that more tears fell when they left.

Sometimes grown men have to cry.

A whole lotta scratchin' going on

A summer ritual for many kids who grew up in the country was picking blackberries, frequently for a grandparent or a parent, or sometimes to sell to other people.

If the berries were for kinfolks, a bucketful probably earned the picker at least a quarter, which was not bad money at the time.

But like most jobs it had its downfalls and some of them were mitey unpleasant.

My family owned about 15 acres outside of Wickliffe.

It was a much bigger farm during the heyday of my great-grandfather Jones, but the family gradually sold off pieces to help cope with the Depression.

On the flat top of a small hill on the edge of the property adjoining the Horn farm, there was a field bordered by a fence row with lots of blackberry bushes.

Near one end of the field there was a hickory tree which attracted squirrels when the nuts were ready to eat. I did my first squirrel hunting at that tree with a .410 borrowed from my cousin George.

Hunting aside, my most frequent reason for being there was the blackberries.

My grandmother, Edna Jones Culver, would send me to pick her a bucket of berries, and my mother also wanted some during berry season.

Both of them would convert the berries into cobblers or jams or jellies, and few treats are better than a good cobbler or a jar of jam made from freshly picked blackberries.

There were two hazards that went along with blackberry picking. One of them was the briars that grew on the vines. A bucket of blackberries went hand-in-hand (or wrist-in-briar) with a scratched-up forearm.

But those weren't the worst scratches. Nope, not by a long shot.

If you've picked berries, you know what I'm talking about.

Along about blackberry season, you could tell who had been picking. They were the ones constantly scratching their crotches.

I don't know if chiggers hang out on the berry vines or if they just lurk on the grass that a picker has to walk through to get to the vines.

Wherever their origin, chiggers and blackberries go together like biscuits and gravy.

We didn't have a good bug repellent back then. It was a matter of "picker beware."

Chiggers look for tight spaces, like at the tops of your socks or inside your underwear.

It's hard to believe how anything that small can itch that bad.

Near the end of my blackberry picking days I figured out a way to avoid the scratches. I put a nail into the sawed-off end of a broom handle and bent the nail into a hook.

I could use the hook to reach into the thickest growth, grab a vine, and pull it toward me. That made it possible to avoid the briar scratches but I never discovered how to avoid the chigger scratching.

Actually, I did find a way. Pod had some grapes and blackberries growing near her house in Monkey's Eyebrow. She kept the grass mowed and the vines didn't have briars.

You could pick and eat to your stomach's content and not get either kind of scratch.

But you know, I think maybe they tasted a little better when I had to endure pain and suffering to get them.

A memorable Christmas dinner

With Thanksgiving a couple of days behind us and the shopping frenzy well under way as Christmas approaches, I was thinking this morning of one of my most memorable Christmas meals – hamburgers.

This goes back probably to sometime in the 1980s when I was living in Oak Ridge, Tennessee. My son Joe Ray was living with me at the time.

Our family usually gathered at my parents' home on Christmas day to enjoy the annual Christmas feast my mother prepared, with the help of my sisters Jeanne and Julie.

This particular year I decided to do something different, even though it didn't set well with mother who expected that all of her children should gather at her house on Christmas and gorge themselves on her great food.

And it was great, make no mistake about it. Mother and her sister Pod, who often hosted large family gatherings at her home in Monkey's Eyebrow, were two of the best cooks I ever had the gastronomical pleasure of knowing.

Joe Ray and I had discussed Christmas plans and we decided to break with tradition and do our own thing.

About an hour's drive from Oak Ridge, near Spring City in Rhea County, a couple of miles down a gravel road at the top of the hill in Grandview is the Piney Falls natural area.

The Piney Falls area was one of my favorite places to go. Even though it's open to the public, it's rare that you run into anyone else.

I used to camp there when Jesse, Jubal and Jolie were little, and we would hike along the trail beside the cliff, winding up at the falls which tumble about 80 feet.

We would build campfires at night and roast wieners and marshmallows and tell scary stories.

Sometimes late in the year, we would wake up in the morning to find snow on the ground and covering our tent.

Joe Ray and I decided we would go to Piney Falls on Christmas day that year and cook hamburgers.

Everyone thought we were "touched" (some people call it "tetched"), a little bit crazy or even more than a little bit but we had made up our minds. We stuck to the plan even though the Christmas season that year, and especially in the Cumberland Mountains where Piney Falls is located, was bitterly cold.

We drove there mid-day Christmas, taking with us the makings of hamburgers and a large cast-iron skillet in which to cook them.

We gathered branches from fallen trees at the site, and eventually got a fire going. I think Joe Ray helped it along with some bar oil from a chain saw.

We fried the burgers in that cast iron skillet over the wood fire, and they became about the finest Christmas meal we ever had.

We walked around the area after we ate. At the top of Piney Falls was a fantastic sight. It was so cold that the water had frozen from the top of the hill all 80 feet to the pool at the bottom. What an amazing winter wonderland it was!

We ate and shivered and admired views while the rest of the family stuffed on ham and turkey and vegetables and desserts in the warmth of my parents' home. To this day, I think ours was the better Christmas dinner.

Daddy and Buddy Hughes proved the experts wrong

It was 1949, the war was over, and daddy and his good friend David Budd Hughes – better known as Buddy – decided they wanted to go into the TV business.

Only problem was, the TV folks didn't want to sell them any TVs.

That was because the TV experts said the TV signal traveled only a certain distance. I think the distance was 100 miles, or it could have been 150. It probably had something to do with the curvature of the Earth and the notion that TV signals go in a straight line and don't conform to curves. Or maybe it was something else.

The closest stations were farther than that from Wickliffe.

St. Louis and Memphis were about 180 miles away and both cities had TV stations, but they were too far away the experts said.

But daddy and Buddy thought the experts were wrong and they set out to prove that they could receive TV signals in Wickliffe.

That's why they began building a TV tower in 1950.

They decided to build it from wood using 8-foot sections of 2x2 lumber because that's how the lumber came from the lumber yard.

The tower was located in the back of the little house my parents rented from Frances Hughes, behind the house she lived in. Fran was Buddy's aunt.

They nailed strategic cross-strips – Xs – inside the tower sections for strength.

They would put a single section into place, climb up it and hoist the next section into place.

They placed temporary steel guy wires as the tower became taller and then permanent ones as it was finished. When it was finished it was 80 feet tall, not much compared to the WPSD TV tower in a field behind my house at Monkey's Eyebrow (it's more than 1,600 feet tall) but extremely impressive when you consider that there was no such thing as a TV tower in Ballard County before daddy and Buddy built theirs.

They had already ordered their antenna from New York and it came in a kit. It was what daddy describes as a "VDX" long distance video antenna. That original aluminum antenna could receive channels 2 through 6. Later, they bought an antenna called a rhombic which was better.

Their first objective was to get TV from St. Louis on Channel 5. They could get other channels later with the same antenna after some adjustments.

The rhombic antenna was pointed toward St. Louis. Buddy used a transit from Japan to point it correctly.

A rhombic antenna consists of some poles placed in a diamond pattern, with wire running from pole to pole. I remember the antenna as taking up much of the field behind the house and the tower. I think it was the key to getting signal from St. Louis.

Mounting the regular antenna onto the tower was no easy – or safe – job. They climbed the tower, daddy on one side and Buddy on the other, and they pulled it up as they climbed. (They didn't use any of the equipment that OSHA requires today for being up so high. Of course, there wasn't an OSHA back then or – who knows – Wickliffe might never have had a TV set.)

Mother says that she doesn't know how she could have handled watching them so she took the easy way out and didn't watch.

Buddy studied the weather maps and checked longitude and latitude so he could figure the best direction to point the antenna.

The tower was finally complete, with antenna on top, so they were ready for TV.

Their first TV was a Motorola seven-inch, black and white of course. Color TV didn't exist back then. I remember that Fran Hughes later had something to simulate color. It was a glass panel set in front of her TV screen and it had three colors, one atop the other. When you looked at the TV through that panel it gave a weak impression of color.

They invited folks to come watch TV for the first time. They set up the seven-incher on Fran's porch, put some chairs in place, and had an ice cream/TV party. This might have been the first tailgate party. The yard was jammed with people who had never seen TV. There were some snowy images, as the viewers watched a St. Louis Cardinals baseball game.

They bought a TV with a 10-inch screen later.

The tower lasted until the big ice storm of 1953.

After that, they were offering aluminum towers which Daddy installed himself. When I was old enough, I climbed just about every roof in Wickliffe to help him put up antennas.

The first TV station anywhere near us was WSIL in Harrisburg, Ill., but it was a UHF station on channel 22, and the antenna didn't work well – if at all – on UHF signal. WSIL changed to channel 3 in 1961.

The first regular station was being built at Cape Girardeau, Mo. We made Sunday drives there to check its progress. That station – KFVS – signed on the air on October 3, 1954. The Paducah station – WPSD – began broadcasting in 1957.

The tower and the TV and the proof that the experts were wrong were probably pretty insignificant things in the broad scheme of the world, but they were big in our small town and in our lives.

Buddy went on to work as an engineer with the E. I. DuPont Company and later operated his own consulting firm for a number of years. He died in 2004 at age 84.

Daddy marked his 93rd birthday on November 1, 2010.

Ballard County's first 'radio station'

The Ballard County telephone book shows two radio stations located in the county, one at Kevil and one at Wickliffe.

Do you know which station in Ballard County was the first to broadcast music and sports?

The answer is, "Neither of those."

To be present at the first radio broadcast that originated in Ballard County, you would have to travel back in time about 75 years, back to 1934, 1935, 1936. Back to when it was still legal to sell beer and liquor in Ballard County, back to when radio was the primary home entertainment medium because there was no television.

You would have to open a door situated between the tavern and restaurant operated by Sis Phillips and the barber shop where Bob Moore cut hair.

J.D. Culver, who later became my father, had been working on radios professionally at his home since he was 13 years old. He lived with his mother, Edna Jones Culver, and his grandparents, Walter Henry Jones and Laura Belle Tackett Jones, at their farm out the Beech Grove Road, where that road intersects with Highway 121 today.

His customers had radios that ran off power supplied by batteries. Some radios in the county were powered by generated electricity but the Jones house was not wired for electricity so Culver, who was a junior in high school, couldn't work on those.

He needed to expand his repair service because more and more radios were plug-in models.

Culver's mother was friends with Wickliffe attorney Haden Owens. Mrs. Culver mentioned to Owens that her son needed shop space with electricity.

Owens' law suite consisted of three rooms above Sis Phillips' tavern and restaurant. Owens was using only two of the rooms, and he agreed to rent the other one to Culver.

"I paid $5 a month for the space," Culver said recently, "and that included electricity." That would have been in 1934 or 1935. Culver graduated from Wickliffe High School in 1936. Culver, who lives in Oak Ridge, Tennessee, with his wife, Jessie Lee Crice Culver, celebrated his 93rd birthday on November 1, 2010.

The power was supplied by a single cord that dropped from the ceiling and had a receptacle to hold a light bulb. Culver had to run extension cords to various strategic points in order to power his shop.

He was about 17 years old at the time, a student at Wickliffe High School and a basketball player on the Wickliffe Blue Tigers team.

North 4th Street today, across from the courthouse, looks very little like it did in the mid 1930s. At that time, Bill Ryan's Standard Oil service station was at the north end of the block. Going south, the next building was the City Meat Market, operated by George and Speed Williamson.

The Rudd-Wear Drug Store was south of that and Bob Moore's barber shop was next door to the drug store. Later, Hilda Kimsey operated Hilda's Beauty Salon where Moore had his shop.

The door that opened to the stairs that led to Owens' law offices was next, and then Sis

Phillips' place. The old Wickliffe Post Office was at the south end of the block, next door to the Hughes & Co. store operated by Jesse Hughes and later by his son, Urban Hughes.

Wickliffe had a movie theater (the Wick) either at the time that Culver opened his radio service or a short time after. The theater was operated by Dodie Stout, and it was adjacent to the Hughes store.

Patrons could get a cold beer at Phillips' and could eat there as well. More than one person has said that the black cook, Cecil Hinchey, made the best, greasiest chili you could find anywhere.

In addition to repairing radios, Culver wired a speaker which he hung outside his shop's window and played St. Louis Cardinals baseball games for people who would sit or stand outside and listen. The games were broadcast by a radio station in St. Louis.

"There was only one radio station in Paducah at that time," Culver said, "WPAD." There were very few radio stations anywhere in the area.

Culver decided to set up his own small radio station. He built a very low-power transmitter and ran a wire from it to serve as his broadcast antenna.

"It was legal back then to set up a station without a license or call letters as long as the signal didn't cross state lines," Culver explained, adding that his "station" didn't have any call letters.

For one of his broadcasts, Culver invited Sis Phillips to come up and speak. After a couple of beers, Phillips and everyone who was in his place of business at the time crowded into Culver's one-room shop where Phillips sang, "Let the Bumblebee Be."

One night, Culver took his transmitter to Wickliffe High School's gym where Wickliffe was playing Barlow or Bardwell. Culver can't remember which.

Because he was on the team, Culver set up the transmitter and microphone and Strother B. "Hop" Hopkins did the play-by-play. There are no records that show how many – or how few – people listened to that broadcast. Culver invited Judge Ben Morris to listen to the broadcast at home and Morris told Culver that he had listened. Billy Bob Crice says he remembers that he and his father, who he called "Pappy," listened to some of the broadcasts over Culver's radio station. "Pappy" was Ballard County jailer and he and his family lived in building that housed the jail at that time.

Walter Hughes and his wife, Sarah, ran a little store near the old Wickliffe school. One incident Culver remembers was the time Hughes came in and said he would pay the princely sum of $5 if Culver would use the speaker to play a broadcast of a political speech given by the candidate Walter favored, but who was not the favorite candidate in Wickliffe.

Culver agreed, but accidentally tuned to the wrong station and broadcast a statement made by the other candidate. Quite a few people gathered outside to listen. By the time that candidate finished and Culver tuned in the correct station, most of the people drifted away because they had heard the candidate they favored. Hughes paid the $5 anyway.

Culver paid his way through high school with profit from his radio business. He earned enough to buy his class ring and graduation clothes in 1936.

Later he opened a shop on Court Street across the street from the old Swain Hotel, but he had to give that up when he was drafted into the army during World War II. Fred Byassee then moved into that space and operated a barber shop there for years.

Politics to the grave ... and beyond

One funeral home buried most of my Crice relatives and ancestors, but not my granddaddy. I'll tell you about it.

The Crices were Democrats.

My grandfather, Robert F. Crice, was born in 1867. He was a staunch Democrat, the kind people used to call Yellow Dog Democrats because they would vote for a yellow dog if it ran as a Democrat.

He took his politics seriously. Today, some of my relatives are Republicans. It's probably good that granddaddy didn't live to see that.

After several years of farming, including shearing sheep, he ran for the office of Ballard County jailer, and was elected four times.

In 1949, during his final term as jailer he fell down the courthouse steps and suffered injuries that included broken bones.

He lived about a month after that fall.

Probably knowing that he wouldn't live much longer, he got his wife and his son Billy Bob to his bedside.

Billy Bob, who claims never to have voted for anyone who wasn't running as a Democrat, tells the story this way. He and his brothers and sisters called their father "Pappy" (and it often sounded like they were saying "Pipey") and their mother "Mammy" (often sounding like "Mimey").

According to Billy Bob, "Pappy told Mammy and me that he knew Percy Jones (who had a funeral home at La Center) had buried most of the Crices, but we had better not let Mr. Jones bury him because Jones is a Republican. You've got to find a Democrat to handle my burial," granddaddy said.

Now that's serious politics.

Grave witching at Crice Cemetery

"Here's the head of another grave," says Leon Todd on this early Wednesday afternoon at the

Crice Cemetery in the Oscar/Barlow bottoms. The weather is cooler than it has been, so it's almost possible to breathe in the humid atmosphere that is common here. If you could wring the air, you're pretty sure that water would run out.

"I think that's where John Crice's headstone stood," Kenneth Crice says. "Someone stole it or moved it, but I think it was there."

Donnie Lanier, one of Crice's good friends, has brought a probe: a piece of steel about the diameter of a pencil, three or four feet long, with a steel handle welded at one end to form a letter T. Lanier probes where Todd has indicated would be the head of the grave. The probe hits something that sounds like rock.

Crice and Lanier do some gentle digging a few inches into the ground and sure enough, they find the base of the monument that once marked John Crice's grave. He died in 1866 at age 75. He was Kenneth Crice's great-great grandfather. Kenneth is my first cousin.

That's the 22nd grave Todd has located in the cemetery, which lies on two sides of a lane that runs between weeds and trees. Before he leaves on this 25th day of August, 2010, he has located around 35 graves. Todd indicates where the head and the foot of the graves are, and Crice drives two stakes to mark each grave.

Crice met the Todds – Leon and Fay – at meetings of the Ballard-Carlisle Historical and Genealogical Society. Crice was telling about his work in preserving the Crice Cemetery, and Todd told him about using divining rods to locate graves. The proper term, according to Todd, is dowsing, but many people refer to the practice as grave witching. That's consistent with the term "water witching" which refers to the practice of locating underground water.

Todd agreed to come to the Crice Cemetery to help determine how many people are buried there. The markers go back into the 1800s. There are not many markers, but Kenneth Crice suspected that many people were buried in graves that weren't marked or the monuments were stolen or lost over the more than a century that the land has served as a cemetery.

The Todds live about three and a half miles west of Bardwell on Highway 123.

They've been dowsing for graves for about three years. Both of them say they can locate graves, but Leon does most of the dowsing.

"I got interested in it after I'd read about it," he says. "There's a lady over at Carbondale, Ill., who's done it for 30 or 40 or 50 years and I talked to her and I just thought I'd try it."

He made his first set of divining rods by bending two welding rods, about nine and a half inches long on the long end and four or five inches on the short end. He cut two sections of a broom handle and drilled a hole into each section. He places the short end of the rod into the hole. The rods turn freely in the holes.

His first set of rods actually is the only set he's ever had.

He says the rods don't have to be of a particular metal. "You can use aluminum or copper or steel," he says, and adds that the handles don't make any difference. "You can use the rods in your hands. You don't even have to have the broom handles," Todd says.

He's never tried to find water, but he says he knows people can dowse for water. "I know my granddad did," Todd says. His grandfather dowsed for water with a forked willow stick.

Todd says that in addition to water, a dowser can find fences, old houses, graves, or abandoned railroad beds.

At the Crice Cemetery, as he walks along and the rods move until they're pointing at each other, he says he's found a fence. He traces the fence to see where it was located on the east side of the road, and then tracks it onto the west side.

He doesn't know how the dowsing works, why it reacts to an old fence line but not to a root that could be growing along that line.

"I don't have a clue. I don't think anybody knows."

After he made his divining rods, Leon and Fay tested them.

"We'd check cemeteries and make sure it'd work," he says. "Some of Fay's people had a stone over at Barlow with five names on it. We went there and found all five graves that were around the stone."

Can most people be successful using divining rods?

"I don't think everybody can," Todd says. "Some don't have the right mindset or something. I think a lot of people could do it if they got the right mindset, and came out here by themselves to kind of get the feel for it. It's something that's unexplained. I don't think anybody knows how it works."

Does anyone doubt that it works? "Yeah, 'til they see it, you know. A lot of people don't think water witching works. I know it'll work because my granddad did it."

Todd says he doesn't locate graves for people very often. He goes out mainly with a cousin who does historical research in Carlisle County. "I've gone with him and found a lot of stuff. We knew it was there but not exactly where. We'd confirm where it was."

According to Todd, he can tell if the person buried in the grave is a man or woman. "The woman over at Carbondale uses a dowsing rod," he explains. "She holds one out and if it goes around counterclockwise, it's supposed to be a woman and if it goes clockwise it's supposed to be a man."

Todd uses a ring tied on one end of a string, but he says you can use just about any metal, even a metal washer. He holds the string and ring above the grave. When it starts rotating in a circle, a clockwise rotation is a man.

He determines if the grave belongs to a child by the length of it. A child's grave is shorter.

Crice knew there were more burials in this cemetery than there were markers, but he is surprised by the number of sites Todd locates.

This family cemetery could have been lost to family members except for the work Crice put in. His brother, Robert, has helped, and Lanier has also helped, but mostly it's Crice working alone to keep the weeds down and to maintain the cemetery as well as he can.

Many people consider cemetery preservation to be very important for family members and genealogical researchers. One person came from Michigan to see the Crice Cemetery because he was a distant relative of the Crices and he had heard that some of them were buried there. Seeing the cemetery and the monuments was a moving experience to him.

Serving hard times at the jail

Few rooms for several people, no hot water, an outhouse instead of a commode, fear of snakes. Life wasn't easy for my mother, her brothers and sisters, and my grandparents at the Ballard County jail.

I imagine that in most ways it wasn't much different from the conditions many other people endured in this area at that time.

My grandfather, Robert Crice, was elected Ballard County jailer four times. The jail and the family quarters were housed in the same building, which was already old when my family lived there for more than 20 years.

You walked up steps from the street and entered through the front door after passing through a screened-in porch. Once inside, the living room was on the left. If, instead of turning left you walked a few steps farther, you would turn left down another hall and the men's cells were down there. If you turned right at the living room there was another room where my grandparents slept. Mostly I remember that there was an iron stove in that room. The kitchen was beyond that room.

If instead of turning into either room or going to the men's cells, you walked up the steps in front of you, you went to the second floor where there was one room that served as a bedroom, and also on that floor were the cells for women prisoners.

There were some sheds and an outhouse in the back yard.

Mother told me that some of her nine siblings had already moved out on their own by the time the family moved into the jail.

She thinks her sister Thelma lived there for at least part of the time, as did her sisters Pod and Anita Faye, the youngest of the 10 children. Her brother Billy Bob, who was next youngest, also lived there.

Probably by that time Elwood, Gene, Anne, Nellie and Dick weren't living at home.

The living room had a day bed in it, which is probably where Billy Bob slept. The upstairs room served as bedroom for the girls.

There was cold running water in the house, but no heated water. If grandmother wanted to wash clothes or when it was time for baths, they would have to heat water on the stove.

On rare occasions a snake would find its way inside. I remember once when a bunch of owls somehow got inside the screened-in porch.

Mother said she also remembered living somewhere else before they moved to the jail but isn't sure where that was, maybe in Barlow. That house had a rough plank floor which grandmother kept clean by scrubbing it with lye soap. She also swept the dirt yard around the house. Apparently grandmother was very concerned about keeping her family and its surroundings clean. Maybe that's why all 10 of her children survived to become adults.

It had to be rough on my grandmother to raise her family under those conditions and also take care of the prisoners in the jail. She cooked for them every day, along with feeding her family.

I remember spending lots of time there, playing in the house, the cells, the yard and the sheds, but I don't remember any of it as being particularly bad. Maybe I was too young to notice, or maybe it was that it wasn't much different from how many people lived.

In fact, my grandmother Culver – MeMa, I called her – didn't have it any better. Her house, which was built by her parents, was fairly large but it also had no hot water. In fact, it didn't have any running water. Water came from a cistern just off one of the porches.

Heat came from coal stoves. Light came from coal oil lamps.

It wasn't crowded. By the time my memories began to form, only she and her brother Russell Jones lived there. The house had several rooms, about four of which could serve as bedrooms.

But even though my memories of the time at both of those houses are good ones, I don't think I would want to give up the advantages I have and return to those days. I really appreciate a hot shower every morning.

It's good for whatever stings you

Here's how to treat a yellowjacket sting: Take off running and yelling, go to the jail, get grandmother, … oops, forget that. Grandmother's not there anymore.

Oh well, there's still a story to tell.

My cousin George Crice and I spent lots of time together when we were kids, teenagers, and later as grown-ups. We were pretty typical small-town youngsters back in the '50s, exploring every nook, cranny, shed, creek, thicket … well, if it was there, we explored it. We were curious and let our imaginations lead us. Mostly, we didn't get into trouble. Wickliffe was a town of around 900 people, and everyone in town knew you. You weren't just the child of your parents; in some ways, you were a child of the town. If you did something really wrong, someone saw you and either took action or reported to your parents and they took action.

One of our favorite adventures was to creep up on a nest loaded with red wasps – waspers, George called them – throw a rock into the nest and then run like crazy to see if we could avoid getting stung. Mostly we did.

There was a hill in Wickliffe behind the Vance store (and it also was behind my dad's radio and TV store). Folks weren't as protective of the environment in those days. Many of the businesses used the fairly steep hill as a place to throw junk. The Vance store sold groceries in the front part, and the back part was a feed store filled with sacks of livestock feed. The door at the side of the feed store was big enough for a pickup truck to back in and load up with feed. That door was usually open and Mr. Vance didn't seem to mind if a couple of boys occasionally wandered in and lay down on a sack of feed, soaking up smells and dreams.

Some memories are not of events or people, but of smells. The feed store is such a place. To a boy, at least, it was one of the most wonderful mixtures of smells in our small world. A tobacco store where they sell pipe tobacco and cigars is another of the places where the strongest memory is of the smells.

The hill behind the store was an adventurous place. There was a narrow path that led all the way down – or up, depending on which way you were headed – to the creek at the bottom. There were trees on the hill, some with long thorns, some with grapevines growing up into their branches.

George and I could be Indians or cowboys or land-locked pirates on that hill and that path. We could hide from large war parties of Apaches or platoons of enemy soldiers that were very real … at least they were real in our vivid imaginations. We played there often.

I wasn't with George on the day he got into a nest of yellowjackets on the hill.

You probably know about yellowjackets. Keep your distance and they'll leave you alone. Get too close to their nest in the ground, or stumble onto it and they'll swarm you. When they swarm you, they don't bestow gentle kisses lovingly upon you. Nope, they use the other end, the one that has the harpoon in it.

So George had the misfortune of stumbling into the nest on a day I had the good fortune not to be with him. The squadron attacked him and he was pretty well covered with stings. George did the sensible thing. He took off running and yelling and swatting at the yellowjackets. He crossed the street, went up the hill, ran past the courthouse and up the steps to the jail, where grandmother was jailer.

She knew exactly what to do to treat a boy covered with yellowjacket stings. She got out some tobacco – probably a twist of Beeswax because that was what she chewed – put a gob in her mouth and chewed it up to soften it. Then she plastered the soggy tobacco onto the stings. That was a time-honored treatment. May still be as far as I know.

I don't know if the tobacco does much for the stings, but it pretty well drives away friends and foes, and probably makes you forget the stings.

If we got into a yellowjacket nest today, we'd probably go to the hospital or at least to a drug store and buy some pink medicine or some clear gel medicine to put on the stings. That may be effective but it's not nearly as interesting as the chewing tobacco therapy.

Good thing the alphabet didn't stop at I

Ever since Edward Culver (or Collver) the Puritan paddled over from England in 1635 to help found the colony of Dedham, Massachusetts, in 1636 and to establish – along with his wife, Anne Ellis, whom he married in 1638 – the Culver line in the United States, the letter J is the first letter in Culver names with an inordinate frequency.

There are lots of Johns, for instance, in the generations that follow the first Culver in the colonies.

My grandfather Culver was one of the John Culvers. He and my grandmother, Edna Jones Culver, had two sons, John and Joe D. (who is my father).

Daddy married Jessie Lee Crice. Over a span of several years they produced six children, who, starting with me, are named Joe, Jeanne, Jerry, Jeff, Julie and Janie.

Not being one to let traditions end, my seven children are named, in order of birth, Jennifer, Jody, Joe, Jade, Jesse, Jubal and Jolie.

I'm not the only Culver to produce children by more than one wife. One difference is that the Culver men of long ago usually married another woman after the first wife died. In keeping with the custom of the times, sometimes the second wife was the first wife's sister.

None of my several wives died. But the marriages did. More than one person has asked me about being married several times. I usually say that I've been blessed to have been married to sensitive, caring women who came to realize that I deserved better, so they decided to give me a chance to get what I deserved.

But that sounds like a putdown of the ex-wives and I don't intend to say anything bad about any of them. Let's just say that I'm not the easiest person to live with. Hey! Sometimes I even want to run away from myself.

One interesting note about the last three kids, who are known in some circles as the "Duck kids."

That's because of their middle names: Jesse Mallard, Jubal Drake and Jolie Teal.

Don't ask me why. I've loved ducks ever since I became a duck hunter in my teens. I like watching them fly, hearing them quack, seeing them in wildlife art. Their mother was a tolerant woman who went along with the duck middle names.

And the kids don't seem to hate me for naming them after ducks.

How to become a sourdough chef, at least for a little while

There for a while I was one of the great sourdough chefs, but it didn't last for long. My mother probably wishes it never even started.

Anyway, who would have thought that a little bit of sourdough could blow up a jar.

I blame it on Sports Afield. It was my favorite magazine back then when I was in high school. It featured the great fishing writer Jason Lucas. He had a photo spread one time showing how to fly fish. I followed his instructions and had many a happy morning across the road at Bob Baggett's pond before the school bus came.

One issue of the magazine had instructions for making sourdough and recipes for cooking with it. Your mouth would water reading instructions for making sourdough biscuits, pancakes, bread, and probably some other things. Those are the ones I remember. It was pretty simple to get started.

You took a little flour, a packet of yeast and some water. It had to age for a couple of days before it became sourdough.

I don't remember if it gave instructions about how to store it, but I relied on the old faithful Mason jar, the kind people use to can vegetables.

Almost before the saliva had a chance to stop flowing from reading the article, I was ready to cook.

I started with biscuits. And they were mighty fine biscuits, even if they were no thicker than a silver dollar. I guess sourdough biscuits don't rise the way regular buttermilk biscuits do.

Those being a tasty success, even if not thick enough to split open for some butter – but hey, you could put the butter on top! – I graduated to pancakes.

If the biscuits were good, the pancakes were better. The whole family was happy that I had become one of the great sourdough chefs.

But there was this one hot summer day when all of us were gone for some reason. When we came home, mother – who still has one of the great noses of all time, a sense of smell that surpasses even the greatest bloodhound – sniffed and said something like, "What's that smell?"

It took a while to locate it but the smell was coming from the top of the metal kitchen cabinet where I had stored my sourdough with the lid screwed down tight.

Again, who would have thought a little sourdough would blow up a jar?

But that's what had happened.

I suppose the yeast working down there in the flour and water generates some gas. With the lid screwed on tight, there was no place for the gas to go so the jar exploded.

I can't remember the words mother used, but I think they went beyond her initial, "What's that smell?"

And that was the end of my budding career as a sourdough chef. I think the end was accompanied by warnings of bodily harm that would be inflicted on me if I even thought about sourdough again.

Sometime later – probably time measured in years – when my parents replaced the cabinet, the sourdough was still there on the back of it where it had run down and created an awful mess.

But it really wasn't my fault. It wouldn't have happened if it hadn't been for Sports Afield.

Sweating my way back into memories

July 2011

The high temperature has been 90 or more for as far back as I can remember, which, at my age, could mean only as far back as yesterday. I'm pretty sure that the heat has been going on much longer than that, for at least the last umpteen days. I just took a glance at the seven-day forecast and the highs are predicted to remain in the mid-90s for that entire period.

When it's this hot, the best thing to do, if possible, is to stay indoors and let the air conditioner run. I feel sorry for people who have to work, especially those who have to work outside.

On those few occasions when I venture outside to gasp for superheated air, I try to sit in the shade and use body English to sway into every little breeze that blows past. Frequently the breeze is substantial. During the last couple of days, however, even a gusty breeze doesn't feel cool. It's like opening the oven door and feeling the heat roast your face as if it were driven by a bellows.

Sitting in the shade and the breeze, it isn't long before sweat and memories begin to pour, memories that go back more than 60 years to my paternal grandmother's house.

My grandmother was Edna Jones Culver, who lived in the Jones house outside of Wickliffe on what is now Highway 121. I visited her often when I was a child and I spent many nights in the old house, where she and her brother, Milton Russell Jones, had bedrooms on the second floor.

MeMa – that's what I called her – would read to me and we would laugh together at stories.

The house didn't have electricity at that time. Light came from coal oil (kerosene, for you modern folks) lanterns.

In the summertime, the heat was often stifling. This was before air conditioning was a staple of life, even for people who had electricity. Big trees in the front yard provided shade and the open windows let in the occasional breeze, but in the steamy summer, it was so hot that it was difficult to sleep.

I remember lying there in the bed with MeMa while she used one of those little hand fans – probably from a funeral home – to generate a little moving air that made it not quite bearable but just a little less unbearable.

Eventually I would go to sleep and I suppose she would too, and by the time we woke up to start the next day the much cooler morning almost made me believe that the heat had gone away.

It hadn't, of course. It returned with a vengeance as the sun rose higher into the sky, and we would face yet another night of fanning ourselves to sleep.

The day George and I drowned

George and I were watching TV the day we drowned, so we missed out on all the excitement. Meanwhile, my parents were having more than enough excitement to go around.

My cousin George Crice was a year or so younger, and we were together much of the time, playing, getting into things, fishing, and later hunting. His father was Dick Crice, one of mother's brothers, and his mother was Oma Dell Garrett Crice, one of the four children of Joe and Nola Garrett of Wickliffe. Oma Dell's brothers were Clifford (better known as Wart) and Howard, and she had a sister, Rosie.

George and I managed to fish in many of the ponds and creeks in the vicinity of where I grew up at the junction of what is now Highway 121 (I think it was numbered 440 back then) and the Beech Grove Road.

On this particular day we decided to fish in a little creek a couple of miles down the Old Blandville Road. We were young enough that I'm guessing my mother drove us there. To get there, you drove toward Blandville, past Hub Copeland's and Otto Beardsley's farms, both on the left side of the road, and Albert Carpenter's on down the road a way on the right side. Starting at the Carpenter farm, there was a long downhill drive. Hayner Beardsley (at least, that's how we pronounced it but I think his given name probably was Hannah) and Anna Tufts lived in the house on the left at the bottom of the hill.

Maybe a quarter of a mile farther on was a bridge over the creek we planned to fish in. The creek formed the property line of Leroy Dennis' place, just past the bridge. It was a little creek, probably not more than a foot wide in some places, but two or three feet wide beneath the bridge where there was a little pool that might have been a foot or two deep.

It wasn't an impressive looking fishing hole but we had been there before and we usually managed to catch some creek perch and some small (five or six inches long) catfish. We caught some that day, too. It was a hot day, but it was shady under the bridge so we were doing okay.

Then the rain came. Not just a little rain, but one of those West Kentucky gully washers. It rained and rained, but we were under the bridge so we weren't getting wet. But then we noticed that snakes were beginning to be washed down the creek as the water began flowing faster, running down from the nearby hills.

It was probably half an hour later that my mother – a born worrier, one who has the worry gene built in and therefore needs no formal training in worrying – decided she should drive down and pick us up.   But she could get no farther than Anna Tuft's house. Water was over the road that far back from the bridge.

She and Anna waded through the deepening water, through the snakes and the debris and the jetsam and flotsam (I don't know what jetsam and flotsam are, but I've seen the words in books about the ocean and here's a chance to use them), all the way to the bridge. To hear mother tell the story, the water must have been about thigh-deep by then, but I doubt if it was much more than ankle deep. The bridge was under water. The poles we had been fishing with were dangling in the water, hooked onto a nearby fence. We were nowhere in sight.

Anna went to her phone and called daddy, who at that time was working as a TV repairman in Bob Deckard's shop in Cairo, Ill. "Oh J.D., you've got to come home! The boys have drowned!" she reported to my father, who surely was stricken to his heart by the tragic news.

But...

Young we may have been, but we were outdoorsmen or outdoorskids, and not particularly foolish about such things as rising water. When we saw the snakes drifting by we found a stick and marked the edge of the water. Within minutes, the water had swelled out well past the stick, so we knew we shouldn't stay there.

We discarded the cane poles and walked up the hill to Leroy Dennis' house, where – even though we were drenched like the proverbial drownded rats (I know drownded isn't a real word, but that's how we said it and it sounds better than plain old drowned) – they let us in.

We were sitting there watching TV while all the excitement was happening out by the bridge.

I don't remember how we hooked up with mother, and I don't remember what happened after we did. Some things are best forgotten.

But there was an aftermath to the story.

I couldn't find the little metal tackle box we always took fishing. Weeks later, the Dennis family kept noticing a really bad smell out in the shed. It was coming from my tackle box, which we must have left in the shed. We had caught several small fish that day, and we left them in the tackle box. Confined fish and hot Kentucky days aren't a good combination.

George died of cancer a few years ago. I visited him at his daughter's house in Michigan before he died and I told this story. George and I and the other folks in the house had a good laugh about it.

At his funeral, his daughter Shanna asked me to tell the story again. I did.

How girls ended my budding ping pong career
Or ...
Who would have thought a tongue could feel like that

If it hadn't been for Louise Page and Latin I probably would not have enough ex-wives to start a basketball team with a couple left over for subs. And I might still be playing ping pong at Teen Town in Cairo, Ill., except that it's no longer open.

Ah, those were the days. The days of innocence. The days when a bunch of high school boys had all sorts of fun doing things together. The days before girls changed it all.

During our early high school years, my best friend Danny Ryan and I were weekend regulars at the Oriac Teen Town in Cairo. We took on all comers in singles and doubles in ping pong. It was a passion. We even wore white shirts to provide a poor background for our opponents.

Other things were going on there too, but they existed only in the periphery, at the edge of our ping pong commitment. Live bands played. Good live bands made up of some very musically talented young people from Cairo. Boys and girls danced. They seemed to be having fun.

Danny and I played ping pong. We rarely lost, except in singles games against each other.

Meanwhile when we came of age for our driver's licenses, we found many other activities to do with our good friends in our class at Ballard Memorial High School.

We would go to Paducah where they had drive-in restaurants teenagers would cruise around. I believe a couple of the hot spots were Bob's Drive In and the Driver Inn.

There was a brief time when a couple of things were popular. One was a place with batting cages where you could pay a fee and bat at baseballs the machine heaved toward you. Another was trampolines. A couple of places had dug pits in the ground and covered them with trampoline material. For a fee, you could bounce a certain number of minutes on the trampolines. Several of us boys would get together and do those kinds of things.

We also got together occasionally at one or another cabin in the bottoms and had cookouts, maybe with steaks or maybe with catfish. Sometimes we would put out trotlines, build big fires, and sing off-key to the accompaniment of guitars, played badly.

Those years provided some of the greatest fun of my entire life.

But then came Louise Page and Latin class.

The best I can remember, Latin was the only "foreign language" Ballard offered at the time. I'm not sure folks realized it wasn't spoken any more.

Louise Page was the teacher. She also taught English, but I think Latin was her passion. She told us of trips to Rome. Latin didn't seem like a dead language. In retrospect, I probably learned more about the complex rules of English in Latin than I did in English classes.

I really loved Ballard Memorial and my classmates. We had amazingly good teachers, and the best basketball gym in the area.

Our class was small, but close.

I didn't date girls. I was too shy to ask them out, and was having too much fun with ping pong and hunting and trampolines and cookouts and off-key singing and good friends, both boys and girls.

Latin class was especially fun. It was populated with classmates I cared about, and we had great times studying Latin and swapping insults.

The end came because one of Mrs. Page's annual events was the Latin Club banquet. And she required that each person had to bring a date to the party.

I couldn't miss that party because I felt so close to the class, but I didn't know how to go about getting a date. I was too shy to ask a girl out, and the girls I knew best were good friends. You can't ask a friend to go on a date, even one as innocuous as a Latin Club banquet. My memory of the time is that I solved the crisis by secretly passing a note to Latin classmate Brenda Thurman, then and now a very pretty girl/woman with a great smile and good personality.

I think most of us used bedsheets for togas to wear to the event.

Later, with another girl, I experienced my first kiss.

She and I were going to a movie, probably, and on the way we stopped by a Paducah hospital to visit a classmate who was there. On the way up in the elevator, she moved to me and gave me the first non-family kiss I ever had. Wow! Who could have imagined that a tongue would feel like that. I'm woozy now as I remember that elevator ride. I began to suspect at that moment that maybe ping pong wasn't what life was all about.

A couple of other platonic sorts of dates with other girls later, I had the first serious relationship of those years, with a girl who eventually became my first wife. We had a special place we would park after a movie or whatever date we went on. It was near her home, off a side road among some trees. We turned the radio in the 1959 Pontiac to radio station WLS in Chicago, where disk jockey Dick Biondi was a popular DJ on a clear-channel station that played rock and roll music.

One of the musical memories that stays with me is the first time he played the Shirelles singing "Dedicated to the One I Love." The song, the station, the trees, the girl I was with – it all coalesced perfectly to send shivers up and down my body. I still shiver when I hear them sing that song. There have been other girls in the years since then, other music, many life changes, but no song triggers memories like that one does.

Life changed. The guys, each of whom had a girlfriend by then, spent less time together.

Danny and I still hunted and fished and stayed at the cabin from time-to-time, but it wasn't the same. Instead of talking about squirrels, we talked about girls.

I've had other good experiences in my life, some of them great experiences. But the years at Ballard Memorial, the classmates, the activities, the rites of passage, the teachers and the classes, those still rank if not at the very top of my list of best years, then not more than one or two notches down.

And as I age and look back at memories of youth, I can think of the cabins, the wooded parking space in the Pontiac, and that first kiss in the elevator.

And it's all because of Louise Page and Latin.

But you know something, gosh, I sure miss ping pong.

9 DOGS I'VE KNOWN

Most of the stories in this book are about the people of Ballard County. But not all of the stories feature two-legged creatures. Several of them have dogs as the main character.

A free lesson in anatomy

When I began attending law school at the University of Tennessee in 1978, a good friend offered to let me live on his property rent-free.

He was a surgeon and an avid outdoorsman. He had opened a boarding kennel near Oak Ridge, Tennessee, where he also raised, trained and sold Labrador and golden retrievers.

His offer was to let me live in a trailer on a hill overlooking the kennel.

I didn't want to feel like a freeloader, so I volunteered to help out at the kennel on weekends. On Saturdays I helped check in and care for dogs that were brought in for boarding. On Sundays, I cleaned the runs and fed the dogs and cats so no employee would have to come in on Sunday.

At the time, I had dogs of my own, including Puke and Dammit, my pair of Chesapeake Bay retrievers. I also had Dracula, a Doberman pinscher. Puke had a litter of six pups while we were living there.

As a result, I was a frequent customer of one of the local veterinarians, Dr. Mickey McArthur, who had a clinic alongside Oak Ridge Turnpike.

Working at the kennel on weekends gave me the opportunity to get to know quite a few dogs and their owners.

On this particular day I had taken the puppies to Dr. McArthur to have them checked for worms.

Sitting in the waiting room, I recognized a woman who was a regular customer at the boarding kennel.

She and her doctor husband owned a basset hound, a purebred male dog of good quality.

I acknowledged her presence with the dog, whom I'll call George because I can't remember his actual name.

"Well, what are you and George doing here?" I asked. "Is it time for his shots?"

"Oh no," she replied. "I'm here to get George 'fixed'."

Just hearing that kind of talk will make any red-blooded man press his legs together in a reflexive protective response, and it had that effect on me.

"I don't understand why you would do something like that to such a fine specimen of basset masculinity as George," I said to her.

"Well, we keep George in our fenced-in back yard," she explained to me. "There are other dogs in the neighborhood, including some female dogs, and George keeps digging out. He'll dig a hole under the fence and take off, and we have to track him down and bring him back.

"We fill in the hole he dug, but he just digs another one and takes off again. We decided to stop that by having him fixed."

"Lady, he's your dog and I guess you can do whatever you want to him," I told her, "but I gotta tell you ... that ain't what he's diggin' with."

Why the American Kennel Club let me name my dog Dammit

Puke came first. Dammit came later.

During my macho period after I had served in the Army, I rode around with my vicious attack Doberman, Tonga the Avenger. Except that he wasn't vicious, he was a sissy.

Eventually I decided an inanimate weapon might be more effective than the animate sissy weapon, so I bought a Ruger Blackhawk .44 magnum revolver and kept it beneath the front seat of my car. I even took it with me when I joined the Navy and served at Guantanamo Bay.

Time passed and nothing happened to justify my preparation for being accosted by bad guys.

I was visiting my Aunt Nina in Paducah, Ky., and I saw an ad in the local paper, initially known as the Paducah Sun-Democrat but later they dropped the Democrat part and became the Paducah Sun.

Someone in Paducah had a litter of Chesapeake Bay retrievers for sale. I didn't have the money on me to buy one, but I went to a gun dealer and sold the Ruger for enough to buy a pup.

I picked out a female of the deadgrass color. Within the first two or three blocks of our trip home, she threw up three times. Her name was an obvious choice.

Back in Tennessee, I bought a male Chesapeake. He was one of the shades of red or liver. It became time to register him with the American Kennel Club. At that time, the AKC had you give two choices of names. I believe each choice had a total of 25 letters and spaces.

Chesapeakes being a breed of dog that typically produce very independent, hard-headed individuals (which is one of the qualities I admire in the breed), the owner/trainer spends a lot of time saying damn it or dammit.

"Come back here with that training dummy, damn it!" is a frequent shout. "Put down that decoy and go get the duck, damn it!" is something else a trainer might yell at his young Chesapeake.

Naturally I decided to name my male something that he would be accustomed to being called anyway.

It was time to fill out the form. My first choice was Culver's Cocoa Dammit. I don't remember what the second choice was. Imagine my consternation and disappointment when the papers came back from AKC registering my dog with the second choice.

As far as I knew, the AKC would not change its collective mind once it had issued a dog's name, but as the disappointment ate at me I decided to give it a shot anyway, so I wrote a letter to the AKC.

"Dear AKC," I started the letter, opting for the polite, respectful approach instead of an angry, threatening tone which I believed would result in their rejecting my plea.

"I was disappointed to see that you chose my second choice as the name for my Chesapeake," I continued. "I don't think it could be because the name already was taken. I conclude, therefore, that you regard 'Dammit' as a profanity that you won't accept as an official name.

"But let me explain why I chose that name. I live in Oak Ridge, Tennessee, which is near Knoxville, which is the site of the TVA headquarters. Anytime TVA sees a river, they decide they need to dam that river.

"I chose the name 'Dammit' to honor TVA. Therefore, please issue a new registration certificate with that name on it."

I didn't expect the AKC to do it. I was writing to reduce the frustration at not having Dammit as the registered name.

But it wasn't long before I got a new certificate acknowledging the name Culver's Cocoa Dammit as my dog's official name.

I don't know if AKC had ever done that before but it gave me a warm feeling know that when I yelled Dammit, it was both a name and a comment.

Things to avoid when training an attack dog

I got out of the army in 1967 and returned to work at the Cairo Evening Citizen in Cairo, Ill., as sports editor. I made two major purchases: A brand-spanking new Austin-Healey Sprite and a Doberman pinscher.

For those of you unfamiliar with that particular car, it's about as long as a kitchen table with a couple of leaves in it, and seats two people or one person and a Doberman. It's sort of like an MG Midget, if that helps. It's small enough that I recall one time driving in Thebes, Ill., when a large dog ran beside the car and looked down at me.

For those of you unfamiliar with Doberman pinschers ... well, read on.

Being a macho ex-soldier, I wanted a mean dog to help me repel any would-be evil guys. I'd never been attacked by any bad guys, but – hey! – you never know when that first time will come.

The Doberman has a reputation as a bad dog, developed by someone in Germany as a war dog, an attack dog. One look at a Doberman and bad guys stay away.

My particular Doberman turned out to be Tonga the Avenger, and he turned out to be ... well, a sissy. I take a good share of the blame for that. I took the pup Tonga to the office with me every morning, and he slept by my desk. People who came to the newsroom frequently would pet him and play with him, and he became quite gregarious and friendly instead of surly and mean.

We went every evening to the local soft serve ice cream place and had a milk shake each. I held Tonga's for him. His Doberman nose was perfect for getting down to the bottom of a milk shake cup.

I reasoned, however, that although I knew he was a sissy, the bad guys who might attack me wouldn't know that. I reasoned that if I gave the command "Kill!" and a Doberman raced toward him, even the evilest of the evil would take flight.

I taught Tonga to sit and stay. I rolled up an old sock and stuffed it into the toe of another old sock. I would hold the sock to Tonga and command "Kill!" Tonga would grab the sock, growl, shake his head tugging on the sock.

When he became proficient at grabbing, growling and tugging, I told him to "sit, stay" and I took a couple of steps back. I held out the sock and commanded, "Kill!" Tonga leaped at the sock, grabbed, growled and tugged, and I commended his behavior profusely.

After a few days of that, I moved across the room. I commanded, "Kill!" and Tonga raced across the room, leaped through the air, grabbed the sock, growled, and tugged.

He was ready for his first public viewing.

I took him to work at the newspaper the next day and told my good friend Jimmy Wissinger to come outside and help me in a demonstration of the results of my great training to turn Tonga into a protective force.

"Take this stick, walk down to the end of the lot, hold it like it was a gun or knife," I told Jimmy. "Whatever happens, don't panic. Don't race away. Just stand there and hold the stick. You'll be amazed." Jimmy pledged to do just that.

When Jimmy was in place, and Tonga was poised in a sit position at my left side, I gave the command, "Kill!"

Up to that point, I had always trained Tonga alone. He never had worked with someone else holding the thing he was supposed to grab, growl and tug. So, as I didn't have anything in my hand, he jumped up and bit my arm. It brought blood.

Jimmy told me, "That was pretty impressive all right, but I'm not sure why you would train your dog to attack yourself."

What do you name a damp red pig?

I've had several Doberman pinschers. Only one fit the image most people have of a Doberman. Thor was flat out mean.

My first Doberman, Tonga the Avenger, was a sissy.

A couple of Dobermans I bought from the Kimbertal kennel in Pennsylvania were very big dogs, but also were very gentle. One of them, Dracula, would even move aside and share his food bowl with a cat.

But Thor was ... well, Thor was Thor.

I was living in a house my then-wife Judy and I built on the old home place outside of Wickliffe and I was working at the Cairo Evening Citizen as managing editor.

Bill Bowers was police chief of Cairo at the time. Bill and I knew each other from a few years earlier when we both worked as tour guides at the Ancient Buried City, now known as the Wickliffe Mounds.

I had gone to the Cairo police station, which then was located in the granite-walled Customs House, that day, as I did every day, to collect police reports.

Bill approached me and asked if I would like to have his Doberman, officially named Thor's Thunder. I forget the reason he wanted to give him to me. It may have been that Bill and his wife had just had a child and the dog was too large and aggressive. I agreed to take him.

I had a fairly large dog pen behind my house. It was built of six-foot high welded wire. It was divided into two sides by a panel of the wire. One side was Thor's.

Thor got along with me okay. He would walk in the "heel" position on the leash, sit and stay on command. But you couldn't correct Thor by swatting him on the butt with the leash. If you did, his eyes grew steely cold and a low rumble echoed from deep within his chest, a rumble that implied, "Touch me again and you'll lose that arm." He didn't tolerate strangers or most critters.

One day I heard Thor in a fit of mad. When I went outside to check what was happening, Thor was biting at the wire and lunging against it. He was having a fit as a tiny box turtle turtled its way near the pen.

It didn't take a lot to set Thor off.

At that same time I was in my pig phase.

I had built a pig pen just inside the woods and populated it with occasional purchases, usually of recently weaned pigs.

One day someone sold me a small red pig, weighing probably around 10 pounds.

I always named my pigs. I had Big Mama, a sow with eight little piglets; Racehorse, the escape artist who managed to get out of the pen and take off running (motorists sometimes had an amazed look on their faces when they saw me running beside the road, waving a large fish net as I chased Racehorse); Possum, the pig who didn't really look like a pig.

When I came home with the little red pig, it was late in the day and I didn't want to carry it to the pig pen, so I put it in the dog pen on the opposite side from Thor. I hung around for a while to make sure Thor didn't rip a hole in the wire between the two sides, but he didn't even seem to be angry.

In fact, what he did was run back and forth along the dividing wire, stopping every few runs. When he stopped, he raised his leg and peed on the little red pig. It didn't seem to matter where the pig was. Thor was an accurate urinater. He hit the pig every time.

The pig didn't seem to mind. Next morning I took the dampened pig out of the dog pen and relocated him to the pig pen.

He had earned his new name: Fireplug.

10 MUSIC AND MEMORIES

Memories can be triggered by many things: A word. A smell. A sight. Sounds also trigger memories. Many times, when we hear a song, it takes us back into the past.

The three M's: Music, memories, 'motions

Music, memories and emotions are inextricably linked.

Each of us has a song or more likely multiple songs that inevitably trigger intense memories of events that took place while the song provided a bonded backdrop.

Some people who may find it difficult to express their feelings in their own words relay those feelings by quoting words penned by some wise songwriter who may or may not have known that the lyrics he or she was putting onto paper expressed a universally shared sentiment.

When I hear Roy Orbison sing "Only the Lonely" it takes me back to the summer of 1960 and another of those coming-of-age nights, nights that all of us had even though the details may differ slightly.

That was the summer between my junior and senior years at Ballard Memorial High School. It was the summer of my first real job – guiding tours and working in the office at the Ancient Buried City in Wickliffe, an excavation of a community once inhabited by the Mississippian culture, one of the mound builder societies.

It was a tourist attraction owned by the Western Baptist Hospital in Paducah, and operated by George and Cozette Johnson. Today it is known as the Wickliffe Mounds.

I wouldn't trade that experience for anything. It wasn't unusual for a tour guide to be leading a group of 30 people, perhaps even more on busy days. After doing that sort of work for summers and weekends for the next couple of years, and selling admissions and souvenirs when I wasn't guiding, I became very much at ease speaking to audiences.

Another of the guides that summer was a college student named Richard Bradham, a young man from East Prairie, Mo., who was majoring in anthropology at the University of Missouri. He worked there during the summers to earn money for college. He and I became good friends, and I looked up to him because of his love of anthropology and archaeology and his knowledge of both.

In May of that year, Orbison released "Only the Lonely." My parents had purchased a 1959 Pontiac the year before, and I was allowed to drive it, but mostly around town and to school.

Richard invited me to come to East Prairie on a Friday night and hang out with him. With some reluctance, my parents agreed to let me drive to East Prairie, which isn't that far away from Wickliffe by miles, but the trip requires that you drive across two major bridges, the first one spanning the Ohio River between Kentucky and Illinois, and the other, just a few hundred feet away, across the Mississippi River between Illinois and Missouri.

When you're a teenager without a lot of driving experience, crossing those bridges at night is an intimidating thing. Neither bridge is particularly wide, but they seemed even more narrow as I drove across them. I kept hoping I would not meet any semi trucks, but I don't think it's possible to cross either bridge without eventually being side-by-side with a semi. The best thing to do is close your eyes and hope for the best.

I made it to East Prairie and to Richard's house. I don't remember all we did that night, except we did a little "cruising" around East Prairie. That doesn't take long. East Prairie isn't a big town. We listened to the radio in the car and at his house, and for some reason the stations played "Only the Lonely" several times while I was visiting with Richard.

That's really my clearest memory of that night, East Prairie, Roy Orbison and Richard.

I returned home later, went back to Ballard for my senior year and Richard went back to the university.

He drove a Volkswagen Beetle.

Some months after that night when I reported for work at the Ancient Buried City, Mr. or Mrs. Johnson told me that Richard and his Beetle had been in an accident in Columbia, Mo., and Richard had died.

I knew a few other people in my age group who had died in car accidents, and I knew others who would suffer similar fates later, but that death affected me more than most. I had not lost anyone I had shared a job with before, nor anyone who was so much a part of a coming-of-age moment.

I lost a friend and science lost what would have been a great anthropologist.

So, Roy, even though you're gone too, you still sing to me of memories of friends and growing up and loneliness. It's bittersweet, I suppose, but I appreciate so much that you remind me.

Musical approach with the right Technique

I would have been a great rock and roll star except for one minor, insignificant, irrelevant point: I had no talent.

Some people are born with natural singing ability. My voice puts them all to shame. No, that's not right. My voice puts me to shame. I remember once when I was young, probably 10 or younger, and was sitting on the front row at the Wickliffe Baptist Church, probably sitting beside or near Paul Rollins. Paul and his wife Gobel (I'm not sure of the spelling) lived near where I lived with my parents. Paul was the church's song leader. He was a kind man and I thought the world of him.

Whatever the hymn was that morning, I was really belting it out. When Paul returned to the pew, he asked me kindly where I had learned to sing. I probably told him I taught myself.

It wasn't until some years later when I realized how awful my singing voice is and that I can't even come close to carrying a tune, that I knew how kind he had been. He could have just told me not to sing, or at least not to sing so loud.

By the time I was in high school I knew that I was incapable of making a joyful noise unto the Lord. There may have been joy in my heart but when I let it out in song, anyone within hearing range was not uplifted with joy. It's more likely that they experienced anguish.

But high school and rock and roll were happening at about the same time. I remember watching Elvis on his first TV appearances, several consecutive weeks on the Dorsey Brothers show. It wasn't the singing or the moving that touched me, though. It was the guitar playing. I loved guitar then, and still do. All it would take would be an electric guitar, and maybe a few years of singing lessons, and I would be ready to join the ranks of such stars as Elvis, Buddy Holly, Jerry Lee Lewis, Carl Perkins. Fame, glory and fortune were mine to grasp.

I think the song that pushed me past procrastination and into hallucination was Rebel Rouser as performed by Duane Eddy. Oh man, that twangy guitar was talking to me. It was saying, very low and in whispers that no one else could hear, "Joe, Joe, you need to play me." The guitar it whispered me into was a Silvertone, a large electric guitar sold by Sears & Roebuck. It was probably more appropriate for rhythm in a big band than rocking with Duane Eddy, but – hey! – this was the late 1950s and this was rock and roll and this was youth still young enough to have dreams unfettered by reality.

Billy Ed Boyd lived a couple of miles down the road, toward Mayfield. He was one of the sons of Clint and Georgia Mae Boyd. Billy Ed was that greatest of talents – a guitar picker. In retrospect, he wasn't very good at the time – he got much better as he practiced and played – but anyone who even knew how to tune a guitar was someone I could look up to. Not that it mattered much if the guitar was in tune. Honestly, I couldn't tell. In fact, if I ever tried to play a few chords and sing in the privacy of a large forest, I would have to get it very far out of tune so it would come close to matching my voice.

Billy Ed spent a little time with me. He showed me some chords, which I practiced constantly, through the sore finger stage into the callused finger stage. He showed me how to pick something that sounded close to Rebel Rouser, and he showed me a couple of bass licks from some Johnny Cash songs.

With that much skill under my belt, the Silvertone was no longer a proper guitar for an up-and-coming rocker. I was earning some money at the time, guiding tours at the Ancient Buried

City in Wickliffe on weekends. If my memory serves me, I was earning the princely sum of a dollar an hour. That was enough to embolden me to go to the Ray Butts Music Store in Cairo, Ill., to look for a proper instrument.

Ray Butts wasn't quite the genius that Les Paul was, but he was somewhere in the ball park. He had invented a playback recorder for a guitar amplifier that gave an echo effect. Scotty Moore, who played guitar for Elvis, would stop in from time to time to see if Ray had invented anything new. Ray eventually left Cairo and opened a store in Nashville.

I looked around through some Fenders and other guitars, but the one that caught my eye was a double cutaway Rickenbacker, the first one I had ever seen. The next one I saw was a few years later when the Beatles appeared on television. One of them played a Rickenbacker. Mine cost $200, case included, which was a small fortune to me at the time, but all you had to do was look at that Rickenbacker and you knew it was meant for greatness. I wasn't, but it was.

A solid body double cutaway electric Rickenbacker isn't much good without an amplifier, so I asked my dad to make me one. Daddy had been in radio and TV since he was about 13 years old, and he can make just about anything electronic. It took a while but he came up with an amplifer and twin speakers. Later, after Jorgen Ingmann released the guitar song Apache, I knew that a plain amp wasn't enough. I had to add a reverberator to capture that sound. Reverberators weren't a common feature on amps then, so daddy had to do some research. A reverb unit consisted of a metal case which enclosed two long springs and I don't know what else. I think the springs slow down the sound and give a sort of echo, reverberating effect. Anyway, daddy learned how to make one and before long I was on the way with a Rickenbacker guitar, an amp that drove two speakers, and a reverberator so I could play Apache if I ever learned how to play it.

I actually did learn how to play it, or something that sounded close to it, thanks to an evening with Chuck Sowers of Mound City, Ill., a truly remarkable guitar player.

I wish I could remember what drove us to get together, but I can't. All I can remember is that a few of us at Ballard Memorial decided that we should get together and play some music. Carol Wolfe of Kevil, a gifted pianist; Lewis Warford of near Bandana, who had taken trumpet lessons; Gail Parsons of Barlow, who was talented at playing the organ; and I, who had a Rickenbacker guitar, an amp, two speakers and a reverberator, decided we would get together and make music.

We gathered at Gail's house in Barlow because there was a piano and an organ there, and her parents were patient and kind people who could put up with us. So we got together – three pretty good musicians and me – and tried to figure out some songs that all of us could play.

Mr. Parsons got a kick out of me because when we played at his house I would lie on his couch and play my guitar. He thought if I could just learn to play in an upright position and tap my foot, I might become a musician.

We figured out a few songs we could play and decided it was time to have a band and a name. The name we came up with was either the Techniques or the TechNiques. I can't remember if we used the capital N. It wouldn't surprise me if we did because we were ahead of the times. Remember a few years back when the young people wrote everything with alternating capital and small letters? We probably were the ones who set the stage for that.

Sometime later, we got a drum and Junior Vincent became our drummer. We didn't have a drum stand so he would have to prop it up on something.

We played music at a few places to appreciative audiences, most of whom were too old to hear what we played so they couldn't tell if we were good or not. Our repertoire was never very big. That was because of me. I couldn't read music and couldn't play by ear, so I had to learn by watching other people or take coaching from Carol, who didn't know about guitars but she sure knew about music and she could tell me what chords to play.

We composed one original number we called Eulogy, and we liked it.

We never had any record deals and if I recorded any of our music I've lost it over the years, so we haven't left a musical legacy.

In times of nostalgia and melancholy, I wish I had some tapes of when we played together that year. The past becomes more important as we get older, because for many of us that's where the excitement and the creativity and the discovery live.

Hearing our music would be a smiling trip into the past. It's a trip I wish I could take.

ABOUT THE AUTHOR

Born in Wickliffe, Ky., a bunch of years ago, Joe Culver has been in love with Monkey's Eyebrow for a long time, ever since he visited relatives here when he was a youngster. He also loves his native town and county, Wickliffe and Ballard respectively.

Joe's career path was not normal. He has worked as a newspaper reporter, editor, columnist, photographer and publisher. He served in the U.S. Army and later in the U.S. Navy. He worked in a Ford factory near Chicago for a few months until the workers went on strike just about the same time duck season came in, and he never returned to the factory. He has sold insurance and cars. He was the director of public affairs at two national laboratories, the National Energy Technology Laboratory, where his main office was in Morgantown, W.Va., and the Oak Ridge National Laboratory in Tennessee. And he practiced law a couple of times after earning a law degree from the University of Tennessee in Knoxville.

Joe believes he is a product of the stories he heard when he was growing up, stories mostly told by the people who hung out at Bill Ryan's Standard Oil filling station in Wickliffe. The storytelling tradition influenced him tremendously and was an asset, particularly during his time spent working at newspapers.

Retired now, Joe lives on his small 6.25 acre farm in Monkey's Eyebrow.

Made in the USA
Charleston, SC
29 September 2011